a canny use of analogy. Anal
the history of philosophica
through signs; we seek to be *s*
in the world. Aesop's early
gained the power of speech, ;
shown the world around us. F
ogy are best exemplified in the mucn noted story ot his trip to
the baths, as portrayed in *Life of Aesop*:

> While Aesop is on his way there, he runs into a government
> official, who asks Aesop where he is going. Aesop says sim-
> ply, 'I don't know.' This infuriates the official, who insists
> on knowing where Aesop is going. Aesop still refuses to
> answer the question, saying only, 'I don't know.' The offi-
> cial, completely enraged, orders that Aesop be arrested and
> taken to jail. At this point, Aesop explains: 'You see that my
> answer was correct; I did not know that I was going to jail!'
> The government official is so startled by Aesop's display
> of wisdom that he lets him go.
>
> (Laura Gibbs quoting from Francis Barlow, *Life of Aesop*, 1687, in her essay
> *The Wise Fool and the Philosopher*, www.journeytothesea.com)

We can see the same Aesopic wisdom at play repeatedly in
philosophy and literature to this day. There is more than an echo
of the above tale to be found in Herman Melville's *Bartleby, the
Scrivener*, or many of Samuel Beckett's frustrated, post-historical
characters and voices. Again, we see repeated Aesop's stand
against the later Socratic 'know thyself' with a philosophy of
'I would prefer not to'[3] or 'Ever failed. Fail again. Fail better.'[4]
These densely argued modern caterwauls of the 'no' share their
collective genesis in Aesop's first foolishly wise cry of 'I don't
know.'

It is something which will serve as a thread within this brief
history, a thread of the 'no'[5], a refusal to conform, a desire to
deviate from the 'yes' of conformity, the eternal refusal to skip

along gladly. In Aesop's foolishness is hidden the kernel of truth that haunts us all, a deep-rooted fear of the 'no', trauma, the nothingness that surrounds us.

Aesop's gift of speech can be seen as an awakening akin to Nietzsche's Zarathustra. Aesop literally awakens and then delivers with unstoppable energy to the marketplace of society everything that has been hitherto hidden inside of him, locked away deep inside by his muteness. With the gift of speech Aesop is able to communicate to the masses, he is able to deliver his fables to crowds of people, becoming in the process a celebrity – and what's more: a celebrity with a philosophical, moral and ethical body of work to his name.

The work of Aesop

I've mentioned it before, but I seriously can't think of anyone I know who hasn't heard of at least one of Aesop's fables – even if they have never heard of Aesop himself. The fables of Aesop are as enjoyable today as they have ever been. We will probably never know how many of the fables in existence today are Aesop's own original creations, or if he heard them elsewhere and incorporated them into his repertoire. But since there are countless fables in existence today, and as Aesop is our earliest point of reference for most of these fables, it is easiest to start with him.

First and foremost Aesop's fables are simple in structure – not only are they easy to read, they are easy to understand. Although, and is true of some of the – at first glance – simplest literature, this doesn't mean that the fables of Aesop solely concentrate on simple things. Their sheer range and scope is vast, and like the greatest literature they attempt to tackle the bigger themes in a way that invites us in, demanding our closer scrutiny, ultimately hoodwinking us into a sense of wonder.

The basic structure of any Aesopic fable is pretty formulaic and easy to immediately follow. There are basically only two crucial ingredients to the average Aesopic fable: a) the actual events portrayed in any fable must concern themselves with the recognisable characteristics of the animals involved and b) a consistent recognisable link – a characteristic such as fear, or hubris, for example – must act as a conduit between their actions and the moral of the fable. That's pretty much it, the moral of the story is crucial to its understanding, or to the lesson being, or about to be, told. Unlike other forms of rudimentary narrative, say a simple humorous tale, which rely on something as simple as a gag to deliver meaning, fables rely on an intrinsic moral code. This moral can be expressed by the characters in the story, or by the teller of the story. And whereas a punch line ends right there, in its delivery and timing, concluding the anecdote in a moment of high jinks and frivolity, the morals found within many fables deliver to the reader, or listener, a lesson that is expected to be taken for granted, something which is formally set in stone, to be used and referenced as guidance throughout everyday life. The fable lives again and again in the participation; instead of ending on an axis of humour, something that's momentarily amusing and then forgotten, a fable begins, it lives, over and over, with each new encounter.

A fine example of such a fable is 'The Eagle and the Fox', written by Phaedrus:

> *Howe'er exalted in your sphere,*
> *There's something from the mean to fear;*
> *For, if their property you wrong,*
> *The poor's revenge is quick and strong.*

> When on a time an Eagle stole
> The cubs from out a fox's hole,
> And bore them to her young away,
> That they might feast upon the prey –
> The dam pursues the winged thief,
> And deprecates so great a grief;
> But safe upon the lofty tree,
> The Eagle scorn'd the fox's plea.
> With that the Fox perceiv'd at hand
> An altar, whence she snatch'd a brand,

And compassing with flames the wood,
Put her in terror for her brood.
She therefore, lest her house should burn,
Submissive did the cubs return.

(*Poetical Translation of the Fables of Phaedrus by Christopher Smart*,
London, 1765)

Here we see a fable clearly formulated on a duumvirate of social order: those with a high position in life, as exemplified by the eagle, and those with a lower position, as exemplified by the fox. The eagle, due to its lofty position, thinks that it can do pretty much whatever it wants, to whomever it wants, based on its intrinsic belief that those living beneath and inferiorly to it have to systematically put up with its actions – whatever these actions may be. So, the moral of the story here is that one should never underestimate those perceived to be of a lower social position, as their ingenuity could very well strike back.

As can been seen above, the moral of the particular fable is given to the reader at the beginning of the line:

Howe'er exalted in your sphere,
There's something from the mean to fear;
For, if their property you wrong,
The poor's revenge is quick and strong.

This moral, appearing before the fable begins, is called the *promythium*, a moral which always precedes the story (originating from the Greek *pro-mythos*, meaning 'before-story'). The promythium placed as it is here, delivers an immediacy to the fable below. We read on knowing that we are about to learn about what is being said above, we join a contract with the writers of the fable, one which allows us, knowingly or unknowingly, to be guided. We learn our lesson in reading the fable in its entirety. Such methodology was used to help those who wanted to 'thumb through' their collection of fables (either mentally or physically) in order to locate the appropriate fable for the appropriate moment.

In contrast there are many of Aesop's fables that end in their moral lesson. An *epimythium* (Greek *epi-mythos*, meaning 'after-story') is something that has usually been added by the teller of the story or fable after it has finished, in order to fully explain to the listener the moral, or the lesson to be gleaned from it. The epimythium is the final link between the audience, the teller and the fable. It is the final part of the contract, the bit to be taken away and used to improve the lives of the listeners or readers. For example, such a contract is evident in 'The Horse, Hunter and Stag':

A quarrel had arisen between the Horse and the Stag, so the Horse came to a Hunter to ask his help to take revenge on the Stag. The Hunter agreed, but said: 'If you desire to con-quer the Stag, you must permit me to place this piece of iron between your jaws, so that I may guide you with these reins, and allow this saddle to be placed upon your back so that I may keep steady upon you as we follow after the enemy.' The Horse agreed to the conditions, and the Hunter soon saddled and bridled him. Then with the aid of the Hunter the Horse soon overcame the Stag, and said to the Hunter: 'Now, get off, and remove those things from my mouth and back.'

'Not so fast, friend,' said the Hunter. 'I have now got you under bit and spur, and prefer to keep you as you are at present.'

If you allow men to use you for your own purposes, they will use you for theirs

(*Aesop's Fables*, trans. Joseph Jacobs, Macmillan & Co., 1894)

The epimythium displayed in the above fable openly addresses the foregoing story, helping the listener or reader to leave with the moral lesson to be learned. The epimythium, only differing from the promythium due to its appearance at the end of each fable, is all the more direct and commanding because of its position. The epimythium acts as the signature of the contract between listener and teller, after this has been received, we are free to walk away enriched and revitalised.

Later in history, as the fable began to evolve into a written genre, the moral messages contained within became ever more sophisticated. The author soon became more important than the fable itself, and it was the author's interpretation of a fable that was sought by the reader rather than solely the meaning of the fable itself. Such rewriting became crucial to the development of the genre, producing many styles and variants of the classic Aesop tales. Eventually, as a result of this new transcribed and interpreted direction, came what is known as the *endomythium* (Greek *endo-mythos*, meaning 'inside-story'), where the moral or lesson is contained within the structure of the fable itself. The most sophisticated examples contain the promythium, epimythium and endomythium within the structure of the fable and are openly used to bounce the author's own moral implications into a realm of supreme social and literary importance. Morals outside of the story were either seconded or contradicted by the author's final epimythium, or promythiums were used to show how wrong some fables' message can be, as a lesson that not everything you hear is to be considered as true. It is clear to any reader nowadays that authors were experimenting in ways of using the written word to manipulate and hoodwink a naive reader into complete and utter subordination and awe. Authors were beginning to think about structure, and the omniscient orchestration of fables as a work of literature rather than a form of social instruction – thus becoming prophets themselves and experiencing a form of popularity akin to celebrity worship today. Reading 'The Fox and the Crow' we can immediately see this distinction:

His folly in repentance ends,
Who to a flatt'ring knave attends.

A crow, her hunger to appease,
Had from a window stolen some cheese,
And sitting on a lofty pine
In state, was just about to dine
This when a fox observed below,
He thus harangues the foolish Crow
'Lady how beauteous to the view
'Those glossy plumes of sable hue!
Thy features how divinely fair!
With what a shape and what an air!
You'd but frame your voice to sing,
You'd have no rival on the wing.'
But she now willing to display
Her talents in the vocal way
Let go the cheese of luscious taste,
Which Reynard seiz'd with greedy haste.

The grudging dupe now sees at last,
That for her folly she must fast

(*Poetical Translation of the Fables of Phaedrus by Christopher Smart*,
London, 1765)

The fox's sly assertion that one should only use one's voice if one
has the thought to back it up is reinforced by both the author's
promythium and his epimythium. The enjoyment for the reader
is the result of a well-timed and amusing endomythium, a
proclamation that could be easily anticipated: '*You'd but frame
your voice to sing,/You'd have no rival on the wing.*' But this is in
direct opposition to the epimythium: '*The grudging dupe now sees
at last,/That for her folly she must fast.*' There are far more sinister
implications here: whereas the fox asserts the notion of thinking
before speaking, the author puts forward the premise that we are
in danger, that we must be constantly aware of the intention of
others. When we finally compare this to the initial promythium,

'*His folly in repentance ends,/Who to a flatt'ring knave attends*', we can immediately see a progression of intention ('repentance ends'). The final reckoning is one of physical danger. The author wants to eschew the light-heartedness of the fox's assertion and manipulate the fable into something with far more nefarious intent ('greedy haste') – giving the fable's reader a sense of impending fear. It is a clear example of authorial manipulation, something which became the standard in the rewriting of fables for the many generations of fabulists that followed.

The influence of Aesop

Aesop's influence is wide and far reaching, spanning many, many centuries of political, literary, religious, moral and philosophical doctrine. All of this has naturally filtered down into everyday life. We only have to look at the numerous Aesopic expressions that we still use today in conversation: *the boy who cried wolf, fishing in muddy waters, out of the frying pan and into the fire, the goose that laid the golden egg,* et cetera. And although there are many reasons to read and enjoy each of the fables these popular sayings spring from, along with the strange accounts of their author's life, it's the literary influence that fascinates me the most. Looking back it's poets and writers of prose who have turned to Aesop, long before historians, politicians and philosophers did.

There seem to be many chronologies that document these influences, and many are as accurate as they can be, although it is commonly understood that we will never know for certain who first documented Aesop's work. The following chronology charts his influence from as early as the 8th century BC: from the 8th to the 6th century BC we see the origins of the fable genre in the work of Hesiod, Archilochus and various Buddhist and Indian interpretations. Moving to the 5th to 1st centuries BC we begin to see both written and orated evidence of Aesop's fables in the works of Herodotus, Socrates, Ennius and Diodorus. In the 1st to the 7th century AD new translations and rewritings of Aesop's work appear from Phaedrus and Babrius to Lucian,

Achilles Tatius and Athenaeus, all of whom begin to shed new light on his work, each writing from their own perspective, injecting new styles and interpretations. From the 10th century AD onwards we begin to see further, and far more sophisticated, translations of Aesop's work begin to emerge in Latin and Greek culminating in the more recognisable European translations of Alexander Neckam, Walter of England, Rumi, Odo of Cheriton, John of Sheppey and William Caxton and the familiar 17th century translations of Roger L'Estrange and Jean de la Fontaine. As you can probably guess, it is a vast history, spanning many centuries, languages, cultures and styles.

It is through Phaedrus' first Latin translations of the first century AD that we begin to see the influence and development of Aesop's fables into a written form of narration, as opposed to a solely oratory and mnemonic form. These early verse translations can be seen as the first developments of literary writing.

Phaedrus was a Roman poet and a freeman of Augustus, an early emperor of Rome. It has been agreed, although never proven, that Phaedrus' translations into Latin verse are the earliest-known extant collection of fables. There are 120 verse fables that have survived, and no one really knows how many there could have originally been. Each of the fables is composed in a Latin metre (an Iambic Senarii[6]). Like Aesop, Phaedrus was a former slave and not much, apart from what can be deduced from his verse, is known about his life. It seems his fables made little impact on Roman society, or on later generations of Roman poets. Although many of his fables are addressed to contemporaries of his, sadly nothing is known about them either. In spite of this, Phaedrus' verse fables can be seen as the defining moment when the fable was first used for means other than its moral and philosophical intentions, and we can see, the literary usage of Aesop's fables develop for the first time in antiquity, through Phaedrus' reworkings into verse. For the first time, his translations into Latin verse became an exercise in literary versification and without these technically experimental rhymes the development of literature might have looked slightly different from the way it does today. Phaedrus' verse is a pivotal moment in the history of literature, the way we think about words, the way they are written in the hope to gain a new life in the power of others' imagination. Below is an example of Phaedrus' 'The Hungry Dogs':

A stupid plan that fools project,
Not only will not take effect,
It proves destructive in the end
To those that bungle and pretend.
Some hungry Dogs beheld an hide
Deep sunk beneath the crystal tide,
Which, that they might extract for food,
They strove to drink up all the flood;
But bursten in the desp'rate deed,
They perish'd, ere they could succeed.

(*Poetical Translation of the Fables of Phaedrus by Christopher Smart*, London, 1765)

Here we can get a feel for the poetry contained in Phaedrus' verse. The lines are taut and compact. Yet there is a looseness, a playfulness that had not been seen before. There is a distinct element of rewriting in Phaedrus' fables, a doing away, so to speak, with Aesop's less fulfilling and pious tales. Many of Phaedrus' fables are given happy endings, for instance; where Aesop steers many of his fables towards the brutal and the murderous, in Phaedrus' verse murderous endings are changed to happy ones. It is as if Phaedrus intrinsically knows that in the act of writing down each of Aesop's fables there comes a huge responsibility. His own name, for instance, is forever associated with each. Phaedrus, not unlike most writers, was crushed by such awareness, an awareness of his own audience. This is not to say that the fables of Phaedrus are devoid of cruelty or black humour, especially the type that can be found in most of the traditional Aesopic fables. Such as 'The Mules and the Robbers':

Two laden Mules were on the road –
A charge of money was bestow'd
Upon the one, the other bore
Some sacks of barley – he before,
Proud of his freight, begun to swell,
Stretch'd out his neck, and shook his bell.
The poor one, with an easy pace,
Came on behind a little space –
When on a sudden, from the wood
A gang of thieves before them stood;
And, while the muleteers engage,
Wound the poor creature in their rage:
Eager they seize the golden prize,
But the vile barley-bags despise.
The plunder'd mule was all forlorn,
The other thank'd them for their scorn:
'Tis now my turn the head to toss,
Sustaining neither wound nor loss.'
The low estate's from peril clear,
But wealthy men have much to fear.

(Poetical Translation of the Fables of Phaedrus by Christopher Smart, London, 1765)

More importantly, many of Phaedrus' fables feature Aesop him-self, thus securing the link between the Aesopic tradition and the birth of Literature, as seen here in 'Esop at Play':

As Esop was with boys at play,
And had his nuts as well as they,
A grave Athenian, passing by,

Cast on the sage a scornful eye,
As on a dotard quite bereaved:
Which, when the moralist perceived,
(Rather himself a wit profess'd
Than the poor subject of a jest)
Into the public way he flung
A bow that he had just unstrung:
'There solve, thou conjurer,' he cries,
'The problem, that before thee lies.'
The people throng; he racks his brain,
Nor can the thing enjoin'd explain.
At last he gives it up – the seer
Thus then in triumph made it clear:
'As the tough bow exerts its spring,
A constant tension breaks the string;
But if 'tis let at seasons loose,
You may depend upon its use.'
Thus recreative sports and play
Are good upon a holiday,
And with more spirit they'll pursue
The studies which they shall renew.

(Poetical Translation of the Fables of Phaedrus by Christopher Smart,
London, 1765)

In stark contrast Babrius, a 'Hellenised Roman', was known both
for his brevity and humour, translating into Greek verse and
prose what is commonly agreed to be the most Aesopic collection of fables in antiquity. As can be seen below, Babrius could
get to the point rather swiftly, as exemplified in his fable 'The
Arab and the Camel':

An Arab camel-driver, after completing the loading of his
Camel, asked him which he would like best, to go up
hill or down. The poor beast replied, not without a touch

of reason: 'Why do you ask me? Is it that the level way through the desert is closed?'

(Babrius, trans., George Fyler Townsend, www.ancienthistory.about.com)

It doesn't come as any surprise to learn that even less is known about Babrius' life than that of his Latin counterpart Phaedrus. It is thought that he spent much of his life in Cilicia in the late first century AD. And that's pretty much it, really. Cilicia (part of modern-day Turkey) extended along the Mediterranean coast and Babrius, whose gentile name was possibly Valerius, was thought to have lived in the east, probably in or near Syria, where the fables seem first to have gained in popularity. Babrius' fables were written in a verse form popular in that area – a style called *choliambics*.[7] His fables were later collected in the *Athoan Codex* which was thought to have been compiled around the tenth century. It comprised of over 120 fables, arranged alphabetically, mysteriously stopping at 'O'. It is thought that Babrius used Aesop as his sole source, but there also exists a smattering of his fables that cannot be attributed to any extant form. These are thought to have been composed by Babrius himself – giving credence to the idea that the fable had by this time become an accepted literary genre.

About this time symposiastic literature was also beginning to emerge in Greek literary symposiums, where writers such as Plutarch and Xenophon contextualised fables in long, detailed discussions, critiquing style and meaning among themselves. Plutarch, in response to these symposiums, published his *Banquet of the Seven Sages* in which Aesop himself appears as a character:

Aesop too, as it happened, having been sent by Croesus only a short time before on a mission both to Periander and to the god at Delphi, was present at the dinner, seated on a low chair next to Solon, who occupied the place just above. Aesop said: 'A Lydian mule caught sight of his own image reflected in a river, and, suddenly struck with admiration at the beauty and great size of his body, tossed his mane and started to run like a horse, but then, recalling that his sire was an ass, he soon stopped his running, and gave up his pride and animation.' Whereupon Chilon, dropping into Laconian dialect, remarked, 'It's slow ye are, and ye're running on like the mule.'

(Plutarch, *Moralia*, Vol.II, Loeb Classical Library, Harvard University Press, 198, p. 345 449)

It is through accounts like Plutarch's, which may not entirely rely on historical accuracy, that we begin to understand the importance of Aesop in intellectual society. Babrius' fables are just one of many rewritings in Greece that would begin to surface. Due to the later popularity of Phaedrus' fables the Aesopic tradition began to thrive in the Latin Middle Ages and on to Romulus' later prose *paraphrases* of the late tenth century. Although it is not certain that all of Romulus' paraphrases derived from Phaedrus' verses, they still secured not only the name of Phaedrus in literary and philosophical history, but also the influence of Aesop's work itself.

As the influence began to spread, newer versions began to be added to collections, especially those of Babrius and Romulus, and soon enough new styles and content began to surface, reflecting the cultural dilemmas and differences of the age. Romulus' collections soon began to inspire numerous medieval authors, who in turn rewrote older fables, infusing their own wit and wisdom – both cultural and stylistic – to such an extent that numerous collections began to circulate across Europe, most notably in England where collections such as *Romulus Anglicus* and *Romulus Anglicus Cunctis* were very popular amongst the nobility and church.

At this exciting juncture in the development and burgeoning influence of the fable as a literary genre the fables of Odo of Cheriton began to appear. Odo, a cleric, wrote his fables in the thirteenth century, and he is considered to be an important figure in the development of Aesop's work in medieval Latin. Although, unlike the Latin tradition of Phaedrus, Babrius et al., Odo's fables are steeped in the Christian tradition, giving each an allegorically Christian feel that was to play its part in galvanising the moral strength of the church in society. Many of his fables, as a result, were accompanied with lengthy sermons, each of which was longer than the fable itself. Odo is seen by many scholars as a craftsman of the written word, a master storyteller who gave unique attention to the placement of words, imagery and – most importantly in Odo's case – phraseology, lending each the power to convince and command. Yet, his fables aren't perfect, they are often prejudiced against women (the fables of Marie de France, discussed in Part Two, are a perfect antidote), and they also preach against many other religions, most notably Judaism, which are seen by Odo and his contemporaries in the church as a threat to Christian civilisation. In spite of this, Odo's fables are a good example of how far fabulists were able to use their writings to employ persuasion, fear and power upon their readership, as seen below in 'The Cuckoo and the Sparrow':

Against all who rise up in opposition to their benefactors

The cuckoo once placed an egg in a sparrow's nest. And the sparrow indeed nurtured the cuckoo's chick. Then, when he had grown to quite a size and the sparrow came to offer him some food, he opened wide his mouth – and gulped and devoured the sparrow.

Thus many men, though reared and promoted by others, rise up against their benefactors and harass them in various ways. So it is with clerks; once elevated among the canons and archdeacons, they set upon their superiors. For such are the sons of the cuckoo. And when these sons have power, they devour their parents, and brother devours brother simply to get possession of property. Such men are all called Sons of Nero – the emperor who murdered his mother, and his master Seneca as well.

A curse on nurturing such sons! Isaiah 1:2: 'I have brought up children, and exalted them; but they have despised me.'

(The Fables of Odo of Cheriton, trans. John C. Jacobs, Syracuse University Press, 1985)

This is a damning fable that sets out its mission from the very beginning. What is interesting is not that Odo manages to steer the reader away from thinking above his or her station (whilst securing his own, and the church's dominance over them), or that he condemns aspiring clerks in his own church, in the same breath as Rome and its past rulers, as murdering 'Sons of Nero', but that it gives its epimythium, the very last all-important words, to the Bible, thus reaffirming Odo's belief that there is only one voice and that is the voice of his God. Not even Odo is powerful enough to have the last word: that word is Gospel.

Odo is a fine example of a fabulist who is completely in charge of his readership, being himself totally aware of the spell his words can cast. His terse, often brutal diction has been starkly translated to optimum effect. Odo himself was aware of the effect his fables had and as a result often grouped them together thematically, which helped to galvanise a far greater sense of belonging and understanding with his readership. Here is one final example – it's a rather fitting fable – of Odo's manipulative power as a fabulist, 'The Hornet':

Using his wings, the hornet likewise creates a noisy uproar. It's as if he were saying: *'Frai bien, frai bein.'* Then at length, he drives himself into your eye.

Certain men of this sort say: *'Frai bien, frai bien.'* They promise you salve, then drive home a sting; they pledge roses and deliver thorns.

(The Fables of Odo of Cheriton, trans. John C. Jacobs, Syracuse University Press, 1985)

Perhaps the longer-lasting influence, one that all fables are known for today, is the anthropomorphic tradition they have carried throughout the ages. We only have to look at a random list of titles to see why: 'The Wolf and the Lamb', 'The Hare and the Sparrow', 'The Fox and the Crow', 'The Ant and the Dung Beetle', 'The Sow and the Lioness', 'The Donkey and the Mule'. Almost all of Aesop's fables have animals as their main characters. The importance of Aesop's animals cannot go ignored in this context, as his talking animals are, for many, the reason why fables appeal. We cannot really imagine the fables of Aesop without them. They inject a sense of wonder into each tale and immediately hook the reader – we at once feel comfortable with the animals, and as fantastic as it all seems, we still feel a sense of immediate recognition. Aesop was savvy enough, it seems, to understand that by using animals to point out our own petty absurdities and foolishness he would offend us less than if he had used recognisable human figures in the same tales. The fun for the listener was in trying to work out which animal acted like a certain member of the public or even of the family, so recognisable were Aesop's animals' traits. In doing so, not only did this allow the listener a certain distance in order not to cause offence, it also imparted upon the crowd his own intellectual superiority.

Aesop drew from many of the already existing natural-history tales of the ancient world and crammed them into his own tales and scenarios. The myths of the ancient world in Aesop's time were littered with wonderful and bizarre animal imagery. So it was only natural that Aesop should use this symbolic wealth to his own advantage. Without such imagery our own narrative history of the animal kingdom – something we take for granted – would sadly be bereft of the humour, pathos and meaning it now has. We only have to look towards the cartoons of Walt Disney to understand the influence, not only of Aesop, but of the imagery and symbolism of the ancient natural folklore that has been passed down to us from his fables. Today, without such lineage there would be no sly fox, cowardly rabbit, brave lion or proud peacock; we wouldn't sing our 'swan song' or still be a little wary of the 'big bad wolf' as we take a leisurely walk in the woods. Such didactic mirroring in the fables of Aesop, where animals encounter the repetition of the unpredictable on a daily basis (much as we do), reflects back to us our own intrinsic wealth of hopes and fears. Aesop's talking animals are essential to our inherent understanding of our being in the world with those of us, like and unlike, ourselves. It is essential to our *everydayness*, our understanding of time and place, our interaction with the people and things around us. Aesop's animals speak our language; it is Aesop's music to us, and explains why his fables have influenced and still continue to influence so many in all their myriad transformations. It is why, for me at least, the latter part of this book is the most exciting – because who knows where we are headed. Think of this as Aesop's very own 'swan-song':

A certain rich man bought in the market a Goose and a Swan. He fed the one for his table and kept the other for the sake of its song. When the time came for killing the Goose, the cook went to take him at night, when it was dark, and he was not able to distinguish one bird from the other, and he caught the Swan instead of the Goose. The Swan, threatened with death, burst forth into song and thus made himself known by his voice, and preserved his life by his melody.

Sweet words may deliver us from peril, when harsh words would fail.

(Translation unknown, www.litscape.com)

Part Two

Political, Philosophical, Spiritual and Satirical

Marie de France:
gender and satire

As is the case with many of the fabulists I have read, the date and place of birth of Marie de France is open to much conjecture and discussion between scholars. Although her name may suggest otherwise, it isn't known for certain that she was indeed French, even though all of her fables were written in the northern French dialect of Anglo-Norman. It can be argued – and it vehemently has been over the years – that Marie de France belonged to the English aristocracy, who not only notably conducted their courtly business in French but also read and wrote their literatures in French, too.

Her fables are littered with smatterings of vernacular English and French, a mixture of colloquial phrases and sayings, which also might lead us to believe there was a definite English connection. The truth is, we probably will never know. Which doesn't detract in any way from her work, which includes some of the finest examples of the literary fable I have read.

What can be said, however, is that Marie de France was a true artist, a dedicated practitioner of her craft – and what I find even more remarkable about the work of Marie de France is that she was allowed such a prominent voice at all, considering the ghastly treatment of women in the Middle Ages. It is staggering that a woman could exist at such a public level – especially a woman with a startlingly unique voice such as hers. Above all, and I feel this to be crucial in the literary development of the fable, is the fact that Marie de France was primarily a secular author.

Her *Ysopet* fables (literally meaning 'little Aesop') were published to great acclaim and remained hugely influential for many, many years. It is thought she translated her *Ysopet* from an ancient English text (erroneously attributing it to Alfred the Great, whom she said, in turn, had translated it from the Latin verses of Phaedrus). Where her brilliant collection differs from most (there are 103 fables in total) is that many of its items are influenced by ancient Jewish and Oriental sources rather than the usual Greek or Latin styles that were readily available for translation at that time. Her collection develops its own style by cleverly synthesizing from varying cultures to create a voice unlike anything that had been written before. In many ways Marie de France was a stylistic innovator as much as a social provocateur. Many of these new fables, rather than being created to instruct or to impart wisdom, were written to amuse; collected together for their humour, they were designed to titillate the reader rather than stamp home some antiquated moral code. For this reason her collection was popular with the poor and uneducated as much as it was with the ruling class – her fables notably poked fun at both – and *Ysopet* was perceived to be rather revolutionary because of this. In spite of her probable connections with the elite, her progress as the predominant social poet and commentator of her day didn't seem to be halted. In his introduction to his poem on the life of St Edmund, Denis Pyramus spoke rather highly of Marie de France, pointing out that 'she is much praised by counts, barons and knights, and they are fond of her writing, and have them read'.[8]

The *Ysopet* can be described as adaptations of popular fables, rather than straight translations, recasting each to suit and reflect (as she saw it) not only her own social world but the world around her, producing fables that were 'suited for lay folk' and much as they were the gentry. In synthesizing the fables in this manner and creating the new from the old, Marie de France fostered a voice that reflected her times, both observing from within and afar, whilst mirroring twelfth-century culture and society from the courts to the city streets. Many of her fables, like society around her, were hierarchical in structure, and animals, to symbolise such hierarchs, were allocated their position and 'place' within the social constructs of each verse. Animals such as the dog, ox, ass and fowls were used by Marie de France to depict the lower echelons of society, whilst the predators of the animal kingdom were used to depict the nobility, whose main activities were war and hunting. The lords and kings depicted in her fables were the war horses, lions and eagles, towards which the ox, dogs and the ass must show obedience at all times. Yet, within such order is the distinct glint of disorder. The twelfth century was less stable than some would have liked and the kings, lords and noblemen didn't rule as well as many thought they should, often treating those below them with contempt.

The noble beast that Marie de France used to symbolise such behaviour to the majority of people was the wolf. The anthropomorphic symbol that looms large in many of her tales, it denotes all that is dishonest, greedy, disruptive and violent. On many occasions in ancient fables, lions were depicted as nefarious creatures; Marie de France would purposely rewrite these, often replacing the lion (signifying nobility) with a wolf. Her famous fable 'The Priest and the Wolf'[9] begins light-heartedly enough and relates the foolish scenario of an impatient priest trying to teach a wolf the alphabet. But it soon becomes apparent that the wolf, as much as the priest, would rather be off doing other things. Such to-ing and fro-ing, especially from the priest, battling with his real work and pious yearnings, are not the sole focus of this fable and Marie de France's gaze falls unremittingly upon the wolf, who is immediately depicted as 'guileful' and 'grim' – but, in a subtle turn, it is the wolf's underlying hypocrisy that soon becomes apparent.

There was once a priest who wished to see
If he could teach the wolf his ABC.
'A,' Said the priest; the wolf said 'A,'
And grinned in a grim and guileful way.

The wolf speaks before he thinks, and his hypocrisy becomes ever more evident, as the priest pushes him to repeat each letter of the alphabet.

'B,' Said the priest, 'and say it with me.'
'B,' Said the wolf, 'the letter I see.'
'C,' Said the priest, 'keep on just so.'
'C,' Said the wolf, 'don't be so slow.'
Remarked the priest: 'come, go on now.'
And the wolf replied: 'I don't know how.'
'Then see how it looks and spell it out.'
'Lamb, lamb, it means without a doubt.'

The wolf is clearly thinking through his stomach, and has been all along, and probably always will be. The wolf's hypocrisy is self-evident: no matter how much he tries to hoodwink the priest, the bloody reality of the the wolf's intentions will reveal itself eventually. Even the phonetics of speech and diction cannot hide this fact, and the priest, rather cunningly, has known this all along.

'Beware,' Said the priest, 'or you'll get a blow,
For your mouth with your thoughts doth overflow.'
And thus it haps oft times to each,
That his secret thought is by his speech
Revealed, and, ere he is aware,
Is out of his lips and in the air.

The meaning at work here is evident to anyone: do not believe everything people say, they are often thinking about something else. Marie de France's wolf reveals to us, the duplicity of those who have ulterior motives, or those who cannot escape their true desires; as the epimythium tells us 'his secret thought' is revealed in 'speech'. Such secrets will always be revealed when thought and common sense are eclipsed by the act of speech.

Marie de France's fables not only dealt with common contradictions within the pre-Freudian collective human psyche, they also took on the common themes of the day – it was hard to ignore the prevalence of deceit and mistrust in her society, especially in the courts of the nobility. Fables such as 'The Priest and the Wolf' were solely created to reflect this. Yet, in homing in on these particular issues, albeit with skill and ingenuity, there evolves a universality that attaches itself to the work and we, as readers in the twenty-first century, can immediately recognise traits within them that are as relevant today as they were back then. This is down to Marie de France's skills, not only as a poet and writer, but as a social commentator and journalist, able to pick up and trace each of the common themes that build to form the make-up of society; the unwavering, stoic human characteristics that are the same now as they always have been. Like all great writers, Marie de France was able to decipher the codes that were already there to use.

Codes of class, hierarchy and subordination were rarely eschewed. In 'A Fable on Choosing Subordinates'[10] the eagle and the hawk are played off against one another.

The king of all birds is the eagle;
His strength and virtue make him regal.
The hawk is the eagle's seneschal.
He is, however, less than loyal.

The fable continues in this rather jolly, matter-of-fact manner until we are told that 'when the heat bothers him', the eagle 'perches upon a high oak limb' and the hawk 'sits farther down the oak'.

The eagle is soon 'provoked / By doves down there who fly around / And play together on the ground.' As the eagle sits high and mighty the hawk takes it upon himself to warn the 'frolicking' doves.

But if the eagle, who's our king,
Would go away from here, if he
Would fly off to another tree,
Your game would go another way –
For I would have with you fair play.

It is surprising to learn that the fable does not end here. Marie de France herself has the final word, in a cutting epimythium that serves to warn of corruption and disloyalty amongst the ruling class.

Therefore, a prince ought not to want
A seneschal who's arrogant
Or greedy or of lying word –
Unless he wants him as his lord.

Along with this concern for social satire comes a unique sense of the political, the fabulous and the grotesque. Most of her fables are cut with an absurdist edge and are dripping in black humour. In 'The Man and the Wife who Quarrelled', for example, a peasant husband cuts out his wife's tongue after an argument, only for her to continue her bickering with him in sign language. In the translation below nothing is lost of Marie de France's acerbic wit and brio:

A peasant had a wife who was very contrary. One day they went together to amuse themselves in a meadow. The man said to the wife that he'd never seen a meadow cut like that with a scythe. She quickly retorted, 'It was rather cut with shears.' The man said, 'With a scythe.' 'It was sheared,' answered the wife. The man got angry. 'You're absolutely mad,' he said, 'this grass was cut with a scythe. But you are so despicable and so crazy that you have to have the last word. Out of meanness you want to dispute my word and have the best of me.' The man threw her to the ground and cut out her tongue. Then he asked her what she thought and meant, whether the meadow was cut with a scythe or with shears. Since she couldn't talk, she made signs to him with her fingers that shears had cut it, and not a scythe.

(*The fables of Marie de France: An English translation*, trans. Mary Lou Martin, Summa Publications, 1984)

Symbolism, metaphor and meaning are purposely all-pervasive here; they are apparent, and nothing is hidden. We can easily read this as a strangely violent and macabre tale, that is at the same time funny and odd in its bloody, visceral nature. But there is also something else meant to be gleaned from within: the fable is a retort in itself. It is Marie de France, writing as a woman and responding to the classic, misogynist narratives that flourished in her society, where women's voices were often removed in a myriad violent and grotesque ways. Here, the tables are rather cleverly and adroitly turned and the joke is thrown back at the violent husband, who has no idea that his actions have been curtailed: a woman's voice can never be systematically removed, even with violence. Man's physical dominance cannot crush a woman's intellect. Even more extra-ordinary is that this same joke must have hoodwinked many of her male readers in the courts and across the land, laughing as they surely must have at the absurdist nature of the husband's nefarious actions, rather than reading further into the fable and contemplating the wider message within – how else could these wonderful fables, written by a woman, have not only become and remained so popular, but indeed survived through-out a particularly misogynist period in our early history?

So with this brilliance, we can only return to: *Me numeral pur remembrance: Marie ai num, si sui de France* (I'll give you my name for memory: Marie is my name and I am from France). And it is here that Marie de France signs off, at the end of her *Ysopet*, with an insouciance of Derridian proportions. This signature is all she left in the way of biographical details. But I guess that doesn't really matter, in the grand scheme of the development of the fable the name Marie de France has certainly left its mark. Aside from the ever-so-tantalising appellation 'de France' we have learnt that she was a feminist, well versed in Latin, English and the classics. Obviously she was a highly educated individual, who was also rather oddly knowledgeable about the vernacular language of her day, which could also be found in the popular romances (something she parodied in her *Breton Lais*). And even though she claimed that her fables were translated from other sources, in fact these are her own adaptations of the highest order, a socio-political mirror to the ills, violence and contradictions she witnessed. For this fact alone, putting aside for the moment the myriad other reasons for their popularity, these fables are essential to the growth in rapid socio-cultural and literary importance of the modern fable.

Rumi:
the didactical poetics of spirituality

Aesop's fables were given an altogether new lease of life with the advent of Rumi's Persian translations, in which a spiritual and philosophical understanding was thrust upon them. Though somewhat less didactical than Christian rewritings, Rumi's fables still contain enough spiritual doctrine and scripture to forcibly cajole those who felt they were straying from a righteous path. In his fables, Rumi allowed space for thorough rumination on the bigger philosophical questions, such as the meaning of life. Within his fables Rumi manages to capture the existential quandaries of human existence within a poetic framework of spiritual history, where the law of Sufism and not necessarily Rumi's own thoughts or opinions gives the readers guidance. With Aesop as his blueprint, Rumi was able to create a mystic tradition that is as popular today as it was in the thirteenth century. Many readers of Rumi today have turned to his guidance in the hope that his writing will steer them through the temptations and excesses of globalisation and capitalism.

Jalāl ad-Dīn Muhammad Balkhī (Rumi) was born in 1207 in Wakhish, near Balkh – which was then part of Iran, but is now within modern-day Afghanistan. His knowledge and awareness of Aesop was probably ignited during his stay in the city of Konya, then part of the Roman Empire (it is now in Turkey). Konya wasn't that far from Damascus, and itself being a gateway between the east and west, became a centre of learning. By the time of his death in 1273, Rumi had gathered an eclectic mix of followers. He was buried in Konya, alongside his father, and it is said that people of all nationalities and creeds attended his funeral. Even as his writings are studied by people of many nationalities throughout the globe.

Rumi was essentially an idealist thinker who sought to explain the meaning of the universe both within and around us. Rumi's universe is one with no beginning or end, in which our present is caught within its own infinitude. Nothing, it seems, is finite and all is a continuous moment heading towards the 'Beloved' (God). Like Heraclitus, Plato and Socrates before him, Rumi is another longstanding figure in the history of dialectical thinking. It is his didactic voice that gained him countless readers all over the globe. Through this tradition Rumi became the most important voice in Sufi thought in the Muslim tradition. By the time he was writing poetry and his musings had developed into a persuasive philosophy of his own making, Aesop's fables had already been in existence for over 2,000 years, travelling far and wide, crossing cultural divides and religious boundaries. The Aesopic fables, which are by and large concerned with humanistic matters, are transformed by Rumi into detailed meditations on the nature of man's relationship with God, and more importantly man's obedience before God. Rumi purposely seeks the divine through Aesop and the myths centred around his fables. Whereas Aesop's talking animals work out their differences in easily recognisable humanistic ways, Rumi offers us a theological and philosophical reading of each of his characters' actions and deeds, creating a series of highly influential and esoteric doctrines. A fine example of such a transformation is Rumi's rewriting of Aesop's 'The Farmer and the Snake' (incidentally, many people familiar with rare '60s and Northern Soul will immediately recognise this fable as the inspiration behind Al Wilson's soul classic 'The Snake'):

One Winter a Farmer found a Snake stiff and frozen with cold. He had compassion on it, and taking it up, placed it in his bosom. The Snake was quickly revived by the warmth, and resuming its natural instincts, bit its benefactor, inflicting on him a mortal wound. 'Oh,' cried the Farmer with his last breath, 'I am rightly served for pitying a scoundrel.'

(Aesop's Fables, trans. George Fyler Townsend, www.ancienthistory.about.com)

The above fable is a classic tale in which the lesson to be learnt is revealed to the reader via an endomythium, in which the farmer speaks to the reader, conveying the message directly. In Rumi's later translation of this same fable, the very nature and meaning of the fable is changed drastically:

Listen to this, and hear the mystery inside: A snake-catcher went into the mountains to find a snake. He wanted a friendly pet, and one that would amaze audiences, but he was looking for a reptile, something that has no knowledge of friendship. It was winter. In the deep snow he saw a frighteningly huge dead snake. He was afraid to touch it but he did. In fact, he dragged the thing into Baghdad, hoping people would pay to see it. This is how foolish we've become! A human being is a mountain range! Snakes are fascinated by us! Yet we sell ourselves to look at a dead snake. We are like beautiful satin used to patch burlap. 'Come see the dragon I killed, and hear the adventures!' That's what he announced, and a large crowd came, but the dragon was not dead, just dormant! He set up his show at a crossroads. The ring of gawking rubes got thicker, everybody on tiptoe, men and women, noble and peasant, all packed together unconscious of their differences. It was like the Resurrection! He began to unwind the thick ropes and remove the cloth covering he'd wrapped it so well in. Some little movement. The hot Iraqi sun had woken the terrible life. The people nearest started screaming. Panic! The dragon tore easily and hungrily loose, killing many instantly. The snake-catcher stood there, frozen. 'What have I brought out of the mountains?' The snake braced against a post and crushed the man and consumed him. The snake is your animal-soul. When you bring it into the hot air of your wanting-energy, warmed by that and by the prospect of power and wealth, it does massive damage. Leave it in the snow mountains. Don't expect to oppose it with quietness and sweetness and wishing. The nafs don't respond to those, and they can't be killed. It takes a Moses to deal with such a beast, to lead it back, and make it lie down in the snow. But there was no Moses then. Hundreds of thousands died.

(Mawlānā Jalāl-ad-Dīn Muhammad Rūmī (Rumi), *Masnavi-ye Manavi,* bk iii (ca. 1265); *Rumi: Bridge to the Soul*, trans. Coleman Barks, HarperCollins, 2007)

First, it is interesting to take note of the familiar theological trope used in this fable: it is a threatening cycle of fear, love and knowledge, which hits us at first reading, but it shouldn't really surprise us much; it is symptomatic of the three monotheisms of Judaism, Christianity and Islam and such heavy-handed tropes were already common in most scripture by the time this verse was written. Rumi was more than familiar with the scriptures of Islam and Sufism, and it comes as no surprise that he should rewrite this simple fable in such a manner. Second, reading both in comparison we are struck by Rumi's didactic approach. His new fable is unadulterated instruction, yet it is instruction from above: 'Listen to this!' he says, immediately attracting readers' interest. Rumi posits a notion that this text – which forms part of his greater *Masnavi-ye Manavi,* a series of six volumes comprising over 25,000 verses – is of the utmost spiritual importance, continuing his alluring call: 'and hear the mystery inside'. The effect on the reader is to create a sense of the esoteric, or the other-worldly, something from outside that is being channelled into us, with vim and just cause, as if transcribed by God himself through Rumi's poetic vision. This is no ordinary fable, Rumi has lifted a humdrum tale to transcend mere morals; this is a bugle call to all who'll listen. Rumi has created a complex and foreboding web of spiritual inquiry via a symbolic blueprint already laid out by Aesop. Snake and dragon imagery, as in most religions and myths, is common in Sufi and Muslim texts. The snake and the dragon are used by Sufis to symbolise the *nafs* (self) when it is loosened upon temptation. The nafs have to be tethered by our will, when it is unfrozen it becomes tempted by evil and we will suffer the consequences.

The verse then begins to iterate order and guidance and instruct the reader to keep on the right path. 'The snake,' implores Rumi, 'is your animal-soul. When you bring it into the hot air of your wanting-energy, warmed by that and by the prospect of power and wealth, it does massive damage.' This isn't to be read lightly, it is a severe warning of imminent catastrophe if one does not choose the correct path. It is life-changing stuff that is expected to become a spiritual/life-guide, yet in its brutal instruction lies a spiritual and poetic beauty – there are moments, if we leave its aside spiritual connotations, when we can become wondrously lost in its fabulous construction.

When we compare the two fables it becomes clear that each has become detached from the other and they only share their common, distant root. Rumi has taken the fable in a whole new direction, compared with Aesop's rather rudimentary and childish original. The Aesopic version works as an afterthought, it's anecdotal and chatty. Rumi's version addresses the reader immediately, it is far more energetic and boisterous, as if it is literally shaking us by the collar, begging us to wake up from our collective slumbers. In the two thousand years or so that have passed between the two compositions, things have evidently changed – there is a unique understanding of audience for a start. Rumi's opening lines display all the confidence of a master craftsman at the height of his powers. His composition starts with an unmistakable jolt, straight out of the ether, determined and unbreakable. We sense immediately that there may be danger ahead (as there most certainly is for the farmer). The opening lines are fraught with drama, and disaster is certainly imminent.

> He wanted a friendly pet, and one that would amaze audiences, but he was looking for a reptile, something that has no knowledge of friendship.

Rumi could, and still does, 'amaze audiences' with his brutally poetic and ultimately persuasive verse.

> It was winter.

The scene is set: a cold, barren landscape that needs reawakening. The warmth of human bonding must shift this winter, to help wake the 'dead' from their ignorance.

> 'Come see the dragon I killed, and hear the adventures!'
> That's what he announced, and a large crowd came, but the dragon was not dead, just dormant!

Suddenly we witness a metamorphosis into an amazing creature, the sly awakening of something sinister is stirred in these lines – from a snake appears a dragon, symbolising all that can tempt us. We are hooked, we want to read on, we want to know what happens next, we want to see what will happen to this magnificent creature. Unbeknownst to us, Rumi holds up a mirror before us all, he teases us, elongating the tension, then the snake reappears, uncoiling, slowly, assuredly… 'hungrily loose, killing the man instantly'. It is at this moment that Rumi's fable takes its familiar didactic course – not that we have fully surrendered to his will. Yet we are already caught under Rumi's spell.

In reading Rumi, what we begin to see is a master of didactics transcribed via poetry, myth and philosophy through a prism of storytelling that evolves to transcend its origin. Rumi used the far reaches of the Persian language to full effect, taking all he learnt from his master, and pouring it into his own work – within this veil of didactics lies the essence of Rumi's poetry (he once wrote: 'poetry is like a black cloud; I am the moon hidden behind its veil'). With this in mind, Rumi was able to break as many of the existing rules of Persian language as he wished (he did this often, most notably in the *Dīwān*). Hiding behind the veil of divine rule, Rumi insisted that his poetry and fables existed beyond the realms of mere earthly confines, and that through his instruction we could transcend these boundaries – becoming like the God he instructs we should attain closeness with – truly infinite in the process.

In fact, Rumi's entire oeuvre would not have come to fruition without his deep understanding of the spiritual connection between wisdom and beauty. If the above translation seems rather modern and brutal to our ears then it is because there is an urgency streaming within its core, creating a juxtaposition of brutalism and pure essence, or beauty: the right path is one of incredible beauty, our nafs behold such beauty before us, yet just like 'beautiful satin' we can tear under this pressure. Rumi becomes poetic through such wisdom, creating an atmosphere that is both knowing and encouraging, enabling his words to implore his readers to act, if not at once, then after thorough rumination. 'Don't expect to oppose it with quietness and sweetness and wishing,' he beseeches in 'The Snake Catcher'. Rumi manipulates the reader to take action against the temptation of the snake, the 'animal-soul' which is capable of 'massive damage'. Rumi is warning all those who read him against the corruption of beauty, whilst arguing that beauty should be attained at all times. Beauty then, for Rumi at least, is proof of God's existence; the potential damage is the corruption of our belief in beauty – something which is both beautiful and catastrophic for him to bear. It was essential, in order to achieve equilibrium, that Rumi surround himself with beauty to help keep the snake at bay.

Whereas fabulists such as Marie de France used the fable to highlight the myriad ills and gender imbalance prevalent within twelfth-century society, Rumi looked outwards and used the authority of the fable to reveal the infinite beauty contained in the universe, a universe created by a God who himself was, by Rumi's standards at least, beauty incarnate. The fables, re-worked within Rumi's poetry, verse and writings, transport his readers towards a spiritual zone, where beauty can be attained by a meditative elevation of the present towards an ever-expanding infinity of universal possibilities. Of course, all this comes at a cost, there is just one simple wager: one must be able to truly see this beauty through all possible temptations, in order to ascend towards 'God' and finally transcend all beings – which, as most of us can attest, isn't as simple as it first seems.

William Caxton:
politics, standardisation
and commoditisation

If I'm to progress within this book towards a discussion of the contemporary authors who I feel are carrying on a fabulist tradition through their varied fictions and use of today's technologies such as the internet – as found in Part Four – I simply must mention the unique development of the English language, in a context that galvanises its place in history.

William Caxton was born circa 1422 and became a polymath in his lifetime: a merchant, businessman, diplomat, writer, translator, poet, bookseller and printer to name more than a few. In 1438 he became an apprentice merchant, assisting many of the important figures of his day, including Robert Large, an influential merchant and businessman. In 1445, Caxton moved to Bruges to work as a mercer and to trade with the Merchant Adventurers[11] who had become prominent figures there. In fact, the large amounts of wealth he accumulated during this period helped considerably in establishing his later career as a printer – not to mention the innumerable contacts he made whilst there. With his contacts firmly established and his vast personal fortune secured, it was only a matter of time before he became interested in the newest technologies of the day – amongst them the printing press.

The first book Caxton printed was his own translation (from the French) of the *History of Troy* in 1475. It was considered by many to be a rather bold move, as people were unsure about both these new technologies and just how literate the wider population was. In fact, it was common understanding that practically no one, apart from the ruling classes, was literate in the fifteenth century. Many of the nobility, however, were well-read bibliophiles and collectors – in fact many, including members of the clergy, brought books of their own for Caxton to reprint. This was the very demographic that Caxton was aiming for, so it seemed natural that he would print and sell his own translations of Aesop's fables for – hopefully, via the voice of the church – mass consumption and enjoyment. Caxton's aim, through his press, was not the accumulation of wealth but the dissemination of new knowledge via new technologies. The parallels between what Caxton was doing with the printing press in his day and today's generation of bloggers and writers with the internet are notable: quick, easy, mass dissemination of information. Caxton, like today's internet generation, wanted to reach out to the far-flung corners of society; especially to those who otherwise would not be reading his work via the now-outdated conventional methods previously used. The printing press was the height of technological advance for Caxton and he made full use of it. In doing this, something extraordinary began to happen: the English language, which was hitherto a mishmash of dialects and colloquial pronunciation, suddenly became standardised.

As with most new-fangled things, Caxton was beset with many problems along the way. The English language at this time was riddled with complications, contradictions and anomalies (nothing much has changed, it seems). For example, English was still in the process of completing its seismic shift from the then still audible medieval pronunciations of the day, to a form of linguistic English that is still somewhat recognisable to us today. The English language, as is still the case, was in a state of considerable flux, but for the very first time, due to Caxton's press, the orthography of English could be standardised, and although accents and pronunciations continued to evolve (as they still do today), the grammar and spelling of English gradually became fixed in print.

This not only influenced our understanding of language and the written word, it also fostered our understanding of how the numerous tropes contained in the Aesopic tradition should look in printed English. For the first time we could see, on the page, printed in a standardised form of English that was immediately recognisable to us, the same tropes, symbolism and fantastic elements that we still recognise today. Opinions on Caxton's writing fall into two distinct categories: those which recognise its importance to the early, mass-produced, commercialisation and dissemination of knowledge and literature, and those which find his writing clumsy and ostensibly lacking in craft and the varied skills exemplified by the more refined poets of his day. But the important thing here is that although many poets writing in his time displayed far more eloquence and attention to versification in their work, the chances are nobody was reading them. By contrast, everyone was reading Caxton, especially his political pamphlets and his fables – the latter's fixed simplicity probably contributing to this. With Caxton's press, and his bookshop, we can begin to see the emergence of literature as commodity, as something that can be packaged and sold to eager readers.

If Phaedrus' Latin translations of Aesop's fables galvanised the feel and shape of the poetic and literary Aesopic tradition throughout antiquity, then Caxton's fables firmly solidified their presence in English, setting a standard and, more importantly, a stylistic English methodology for those eager to follow. Not only did his fables promote the radical standardisation of the English language, they also injected a new, modern moral and political stance. Caxton's fables, printing press, translations and pamphlets became of the people and for the people. His work served as a conduit that delivered a package of moral and social instruction. Caxton himself probably introduced many of these new morals himself, as he had already begun to see his press as his own personal mission to instruct society at large, which he felt was rapidly deteriorating all around him.

His fables delivered a ripple of formality and order, which was employed with a firm belief that society needed immediate moral guidance. Caxton, in printing his own fables, was setting such instruction in stone – and more importantly, making it available for future generations to follow.

The history of the fable had, by the time Caxton had set them in print, certainly travelled some distance: from oral tradition to the newer established notion that fables could help shape society both politically and morally. Yet, running alongside this full-steam-ahead progression into the modern was the fable's own literary legacy. If Caxton had galvanised the moral implications of fables for a future generation of readers, he had also governed their stylistic presentation, apropos of how a fable should appear, hereafter, to each reader on the page.

Looking at Caxton's fables now, as they appeared in print, they can seem extremely foreign to us. Take 'Of the sowe and of the wulf', for example:

> It is not good to byleue all suche thynges as men may here / wherof Esope sayth suche a fable / Of a wulf whiche came toward a sowe / whiche wepte and made sorowe for the grete payne that she felte / by cause she wold make her yong pygges / And the wulf came to her sayeng / My suster make thy yong pygges surely / for ioyously and with good wylle / I shalle helpe & serue the / And the sowe sayd thenne to hym / go forth on thy waye / for I haue no nede ne myster of suche a seruaunt / For as long as thow shalt stonde here I shal not delyuere me of my charge / For other thyng thow desyrest not / than to haue and ete them / The wulf thenne wente / and the sowe was anone delyuerd of her pygges / For yf she had byleuyd hym she had done a sorowful byrthe /
>
> *And thus he that folysshly byleueth / folysshly it happeth to hym*

(www.mythfolklore.net)

The Caxton fables follow the Aesopic tradition but differ in their retelling. Caxton's fables are infused with light-heartedness and humour. They are written for mass appeal, but also contain a serious message, as can be seen in 'Of the hawke and of other byrdes':

> The ypocrytes maken to god a berd of strawe / As recyteth to vs this fable / Of a hawke / whiche somtyme fayned / that he wold haue celebred and holden a natall or a grete feste / the whiche fest shold be celebred within a Temple / And to this feste and solempnyte he Inuyted and somoned alle the smal byrdes / to the whiche they came / And Incontynent as they were all come in to the temple / the hauk shette the gate and put them alle to dethe / one after an other /
> *And therfore this fable sheweth to vs / how we must kepe our self fro all them / whiche vnder fayre semynge haue a fals herte / and that ben ypocrytes and deceptours of god and of the world /*
> (www.mythfolklore.net)

It is a fable that pulls no punches. From the very first line Caxton informs his reader of the 'ypocrytes' before God who deceive us with their 'berd of strawe'. Caxton is warning all to be mindful of false gods and the dangers that lie within. We must 'kepe our self fro all them' and avoid a 'fals herte'. Caxton's fables are lessons in following a Christian God, his message is hard-hitting and often straight to the point: these fables are the right path towards God. When we read them now, we can immediately recognise them as works of rhetorical instruction, but they also possess an otherness, a poetic sensibility that still holds great appeal. It is hard to look at the above examples and truly think of them as something that was once cutting edge, but they were. To the new readers who bought Caxton's books the examples above were part of something so modern and revolutionary, that it changed the very nature of literature, not just the written word and the English language. Through these fables we see the emergence of the English language, not how it was spoken, but how it should be printed and disseminated. Through Caxton, English literature had finally come of age, it had reached a point of no return, where things can progress and fall back upon each other, for scholars and writers alike to compare and discuss. Caxton had set the foundations for many of the English-speaking fabulists to follow. But more important than all of this was the fact that fables could now be bought. Fables had, for the very first time, become a commodity that was in demand – suddenly fables were something we could choose to own, to treasure, and to collect.

Jean de la Fontaine:
the versification of philosophy

During his life Jean de la Fontaine was as popular as anyone could be. We might even compare his popularity to that of Walt Disney in his heyday, but that would also be doing La Fontaine a disservice. Although he shared similar fame and influence, his poetry and especially his fables struck a deep philosophical chord as well as managing to keep the mass populace light-heartedly entertained. In fact, it is hard for us to understand today just how popular his verse translations of Aesop's fables became.

La Fontaine's verse translations were purposely loaded with moral and simplistic permutations, which guided and led the mass populace of his day. The architecture of each of his fables was designed in such a way as to give the reader a moral code in a slick and effective manner. This is not to say that La Fontaine didn't have fun writing them, as it is evident that he did, judging by the humour that seeps from each and every one. La Fontaine's insouciance is legendary. His overtly black humour was coupled with a studied nonchalance only a well-loved avuncular figure could produce and constantly get away with writing. At times heavy-handed, his verse can also be light and frivolous (his fable 'Gout and the Spider' is a fine example), and it is understandable that we sometimes forget about the number of plays, poems and politico/literary pamphlets he produced during his lifetime, as we look back at the influence of his fables.

A member of the *Quartet of the Rue du Vieux Colombier*[12] alongside Molière, Racine and Boileau, he was openly regarded by such luminaries as Flaubert as one of the finest poets and thinkers of his generation. La Fontaine was a poet who reinvented the staid rhythms of verse poetry, undoing its hitherto conservative restrictions and allowing the French language to sing freely in his work. Such freeness, or openness of language, in his poetry and fables led to a philosophical universality where language could roam outwards into other realms of expression, or choose to remain tightly observational of metre and versification, both helping to create a feeling of risk and confidence. La Fontaine's fables, in this respect, were works of charismatic beauty and scope. He was essentially a modern poet, who thought outside of the collective norms, creating a voice that was both fresh and distinctive. Reading his fables now they still contain the same vigour and practically zip across the page. They still ring true, we can relate to them, echoing our own sentiments and fears and brio, their surrealism seems familiar to us – it all seems to make perfect sense. Like all great writers (echoing sentiments I mentioned earlier), La Fontaine's faux-simplicity helps to hoodwink us into a sense of familiarity (even if everything mentioned is completely foreign to us), whilst at the same time offering a level of assuredness and earnest composition which seals their moral and literary implications. The work of La Fontaine is as literary as that of the majority of great thinkers who have all helped to foster our understanding of the world around us – and most importantly, our place within it. Put simply, La Fontaine's fables are an essential piece in the literary jigsaw of the Aesopic tradition and its transition into the realms of modern literature.

Although, as with most early fabulists, his fables became commonly known for their religious moralising (his verses were especially popular with Victorian schoolmasters who read them as anti-Darwinian texts), there also lurks something else within much of his verse, if one is to brush aside the Christian ethics and heavy-handed moralising (albeit executed with an avuncular flourish), there can be found a philosophical root that can be left to much interpretation. La Fontaine was well aware of the intellectual history of fables, from the lost attempts of Socrates to create poetry from them, to the rewritings of Archilochus, Aristotle, Plato, Diodorus and Plutarch. La Fontaine was well versed in Aesop's rich history of interpretation. Although it was the fables of Babrius that made the biggest impact in his day, it can be argued that La Fontaine took the fables of Phaedrus as his poetic model during the composition of his own – something that is considered crucial in their vast development (like Phaedrus, La Fontaine takes great care in versification, grammar and tautness whilst managing to free the genre from its traditional shackles).

In 'Death and the Woodman' (here translated from the original French by Gordon Pirie[13]) Sisyphus looms large. To begin, an 'ageing woodman' is walking home from a hard day's work:

He bore a faggot on his back
And groaned beneath its weight.
Halfway, he threw it down, and fell
To musing on his fate.

In 'musing on his fate' we are given the existential conundrum (something that now seems overly familiar to us): what is the point in all this? Why am I here? Who am I? And so on and so forth.

What joy had life afforded him
In all this time on earth?
Since boyhood, what has been his share
Of pleasure, or of mirth?

The woodman works day in, day out to feed his family, and to take care of his 'wife, children, taxes, levies, debts, / And labour for his Lord–'. The heavy burden of this perpetual toil is too much for him, life's weight is pushing him towards the inevitable end.

> *He called for death, who came at once,*
> *And asked him what he wanted:*
> *If it was something death could do,*
> *It should be quickly granted.*

Is the only true answer to the weight of existence in death? Is life just some Sisyphean castigation to be endured, its weight to be shouldered day in, day out? Is it something which can be reprieved by death alone? The lone woodman instigates all these questions for us and gives us his (our universal) answer:

> *The woodman took one look at death,*
> *And quite forgot his pain.*
> *'Please would you help lift this wood*
> *Upon my back again?'*

It seems even death cannot free us from the shackles of existence, we seem riveted to it, the more we try to free ourselves from it the tighter its hold becomes – something we are condemned to endure. La Fontaine gives us his answer in the final stanza, making sure we understand the implications:

> *For ills of body and of mind*
> *Our death's a certain cure;*
> *But nature has a law that bids*
> *Us suffer and endure.*

Just like Sisyphus we are eternally condemned to a life of repetition and suffering. We face the same struggle day after day with the perceived monotony of the rising and falling sun. With each swipe of our identification card each morning at our place of work, as La Fontaine tells us, we are Sisyphus personified.

Like Ovid before him, Kafka (who I'll be discussing in Part Three) and Camus much later, La Fontaine is thinking within this marvellous fable in purely philosophical and literary terms, using the myth of Sisyphus to demonstrate fully man's unconscious subservience to existence itself. What we are witnessing here is something that runs a lot deeper than the surface of a mere moral – we are seeing the fable transformed into a literary device that sparks metaphysical, symbolic and philosophical quandaries for each reader to consider, alongside the usual moral, theological and pious implications we take for granted. For the first time in a modern context we begin to see how a certain genre can be used to shed new light on the philosophical and mythical musings of the past, reigniting them right up to the present.

Of all the fables that Jean de la Fontaine composed, it was 'The Oak and the Reed' (again here translated from the original French by Gordon Pirie[14]) that was said to be his own favourite.

The Oak one day looked down upon the reed,
And said: 'it's not much of a life you lead,
As far as I can see.
You bow your head obsequiously
To every passing breeze.

To further this philosophical exploration of La Fontaine's verse it is hard for many readers to consider these very first lines without being put in mind of Blaise Pascal's own wondrous lines from his *Pensées*:

Man is but a reed, the most feeble thing in nature, but he is a thinking reed.
(Blaise Pascal, *Pensées*, trans. A. Krailsheimer, Penguin Classics, 2003)

La Fontaine is alluding to this 'thinking reed' in the above fable. Although the verse is Aesopic in tradition and subject, it can also be read as a meditation on Pascal's famous maxim. The oak, imperious and stoic, rooted, without much need to ponder the merciless perils of life, imparts its knowledge and presence upon the lowly, feeble reed with dignified vigour.

> 'While I, whose broad and lofty crown
> Makes me undisputed king of trees,
> Withstand the roughest storm with ease;
> And when the summer sun burns fierce,
> My spreading branches make a screen
> Of thick, impenetrable green
> That brightest sunbeams cannot pierce.'

The oak, firmly rooted amongst nature, impenetrable and immovable, is able to withstand any onslaught thrown its way – or so things seem.

> 'Now if you lived beneath my shade,
> You'd have much less to fear; but I'm afraid
> You mostly seem to have to grow
> In wet and windy open places. No,
> I'd say that Mother Nature has been far from kind.'

The mighty oak, huge and colossal in presence, has been hoodwinked by Mother Nature, and the thinking reed is fully aware of the power she can hold. The thinking reed would never fall into such an obvious trap, gladly bowing down. Like Pascal, La Fontaine is aware of our weaknesses; our feeble, finite nature, caught, much like the reed, between the nothingness from which we arise and the finitude which will one day engulf us all.

> 'I'm much obliged, my lord,' replied the reed,
> 'For your concern; but really, there's no need
> To worry. I assure you, I don't mind
> The breezes and the winds. I bow

And bend, but do not break. In fact,
I do believe you ought to fear them more
Than I; for though you haven't cracked
Under their onslaught up to now,
Who knows what greater fury they may have in store?'

La Fontaine has great fun here describing the mighty oak's downfall, dressed up as a moralising sermon, he pokes fun at those who hide behind the foundations that hold them firm in their beliefs. In a stroke of double-edged brio is La Fontaine actually questioning his own readers' beliefs?

No sooner said than from the North
Straight down upon them swept
As wild a wind as any that burst forth
From Aeolus' bag, while tired Ulysses slept.

The thinking reed, unshackled, free from sturdy foundation, is able to free itself within the wind. The reed, caught within the swirling vortex of existence, is able to maintain its dignity, through stealth, in the face of the torrential onslaught.

The reed gave way; the oak stood fast.
The wind blew harder still. At last,
With doubled force, it had its way,
And prone upon the ground, uprooted, lay
The royal tree, whose crown had stood so high
That it had seemed to reach the sky.

La Fontaine, like Pascal before him, knew that we can never fully 'reach the sky' no matter how mighty we seem, or through whatever title we are born into or have thrust upon us. Like Pascal, La Fontaine intrinsically understood man's unique frailty and complete and utter insignificance compared to the greater wonders of existence. Like Pascal's 'thinking reed' he understands that in order to make any semblance of progress one must give way to the onslaught thrown one's way. Such philosophical paradoxes and hidden intertextuality set La Fontaine's work apart from that of other fabulists such as Roger L'Estrange, who, rather than question our being in the world, use the Aesopic tradition to keep people firmly in place.

The symbol of the mighty oak tree is extremely common in Western culture. Often it is used to symbolise strength and endurance. Politically the oak has been used by many political parties, including the Conservatives in the UK. La Fontaine's oak, although rather hubristic and, indeed, conservative in its steadfast refusal to give way (or its lack of acknowledgement that to give way might even be a possibility), can also be seen to symbolise for La Fontaine the great fear of the unknown. His oak, although cocksure and fully aware of its own standing, can be viewed as a sign of weakness in the face of its resolve, while the lowly reed, swaying in the water, in accepting this weakness, is seen by La Fontaine to be showing true strength, both of character and of mind.

Such philosophical undercurrents did not go unnoticed by many literary greats. In James Joyce's *Finnegans Wake*, for instance, La Fontaine's reworking of Aesop's 'The Ant and the Grasshopper' is given a whole new meaning and interpretation in his mesmerising 'The Ondt and the Gracehoper' (I will be discussing Joyce's fable in Part Three).

While Joyce's rewriting is still being written about to this day as scholars attempt to crack its hidden ciphers, La Fontaine's version (again taken from Gordon Pirie's translation from the original French[15]) of the same fable is light and quick to the point, almost as jaunty as the grasshopper's song:

A grasshopper, all summer long,
Had sung without a care;
But when the autumn winds blew strong,
She found her shelves were bare:

The carefree existence of the grasshopper is skilfully laid bare by La Fontaine in the first two lines, where we all recognise the image of song as something that can be considered merry and laid-back: the sun high in the blue sky, the song drifting along the green valley. This image is then quickly replaced by the advent of the 'autumn winds' as they blow cruelly in, leaving nothing to waste.

No fly or grub – never a scrap
Of victuals stored away,
To fill the dreadful hungry gap
From Michaelmas to May.

Here we immediately begin to feel the pain of hunger within the passing of time – the physical cutting into the temporal like a scythe. Although it is time, and not physical hunger, that weighs most heavily in this, one of La Fontaine's most well-loved and popular fables. The passing of time depicted in this verse is four-fold: we see the grasshopper singing without a care in the world all summer long, the busy ant in the following stanza collecting food and labouring all summer long, the months of idleness experienced by the grasshopper, finally resulting in the pain of hunger, or the 'hunger gap' of time, a painful 'gap' in our universe, that hovers over the entire fable like a spectre ready to take the place of time itself. Ultimately, this fourfold combination forces the grasshopper to begin begging the ant for food.

So off she went to see the ant,
Her busy farming neighbour,
Who'd guarded against future want
By unremitting labour.

The 'unremitting labour' within the passing of time is symbolised here, pointing us towards the work we have to put into the very existence of time. It is exemplified by the ant's stance 'against future want': if we work now, then *now* will always be profitable.

The weight of hunger forces the grasshopper to shrug off her present want, as she realises the poverty of her future each and every moment she goes without.

> *'Please let me have a grain or two*
> *To see me through till spring.*
> *I'll pay you back, with interest too,*
> *When next year's harvest's in.'*

Again, we witness the projection of time and the injection of hope within it. The grasshopper is hopeful of 'seeing' herself 'through till spring' via the harvest of the ant's past labour, and a future is born again in the present, from the labour of the past. But, alas, it isn't to be, as the ant questions the grasshopper's motivation:

> *'Tell me, what were you playing at,*
> *While summer days were long?'*

It is at this moment that we begin to imagine the hard labour of the ant, where time, elongated, has dragged his toil across the far reaches of each summer month, the struggle of each day stretching beyond the horizon: time's only point of departure (even if we never reach it). Whereas the grasshopper's summer has effectively ended all too suddenly, it has passed along without being noticed. Time has quickened, as time seems to do when one is supposedly having fun, as we can see in the hungry grasshopper's retort:

> *'Why, in the grasses tall I sat,*
> *And sang my busy song.'*

The grasshopper was 'busy' doing nothing, simply singing and thinking of the present and nothing else, enjoying the ecstasy of the moment. This is something the ant has no time for and such idleness is abhorrent to him. Time itself, it seems, has truly been wasted.

'You sang, you say? How very charming!
Well, summer days are fled,
And since your talents aren't for farming,
You'd better dance instead!'

The obvious temporal space inhabited within this fable is the passing of summer into winter, but we also see glimpses of the past and the future, where the boundaries of each have blurred into one another, causing a cyclical conveyor-belt of toil and struggle, past and present, all colliding with the carefree notion of nothingness, of doing nothing and being nothing, where pleasure is sought to alleviate the passing of time.

Like all great writers of real despair La Fontaine is never far from the succour of humour. His fables practically drip with it; they are often laugh-out-loud funny, strangely peculiar, or just downright stuffed with scathing black humour by the bucket-load. Often they take anthropomorphism to new and surreal levels. The strangely hilarious 'Gout and the Spider' (translated from the original French by Gordon Pirie[16]) is one such fine example. To begin with, the temerity of 'gout' becoming a character in any fable is beyond the realms of good taste even today, but to give it the nobility of character is something else – how can something so nasty and horrid suddenly become a jaunty character within a fable? It is the deliberate juxtaposition here of the horrid and the jaunty that gives this fable its strength.

Gout and the Spider, so the poets tell,
Were born in Hell.
Hell gave them birth,
And brought them up to plague mankind on Earth.

How can the notion of something 'born in hell' and brought up from its fiery depths to 'plague mankind on earth' ever be perceived as humorous? The secret lies in La Fontaine's clever interweaving of playfulness and the grotesque – there is a sense of self-deprecation with which most readers will identify. Gout and the spider are fully grown, and they have nothing to do, so their mother suggests they should each get to work as soon as they possibly can.

> *Their loving parent said: 'My dears,*
> *It's time to think of your careers.*
> *You're old enough to launch out on your own,*
> *And I've no doubt you'll irk*
> *Mankind as soon as you get down to work.'*

We immediately recognise the irksome nature of gout and the spider, both looking closer and turning away from the very thought of their torment. Coupled with the anthropomorphic façade that overlays the whole ordeal we cannot help but laugh at our predicament: their toil is used to cause us as much misery as possible, rich and poor alike.

> *'But first, before you do, let's think where you're to go.*
> *Consider these fine houses, tall and spacious,*
> *Where rich men dwell, and where the living's gracious,*
> *And these mean hovels, cramped and dark and low,*
> *The dwellings of the labouring poor –*
> *These are the quarters you are destined for.'*

It is their shared bumbling, uncertain presence that piques our humour. Both are sent to the wrong households and their irksome presence goes unnoticed. Until they swap places and the humour is revealed, unearthed in our shared recognition of their rightful place and surroundings.

Jean de la Fontaine's fables are crucial as Aesopic translations per se – but far more important to us is his development of the genre into something far more satisfying and far-reaching: La Fontaine's fables gave life to a wider, satirical genre of philosophical writing. Through this sleight of hand he was able to comment on life as he saw it, paving the way for the allegorical tradition in literature and modern thinking. 'Gout and the Spider', whilst displaying its humour, also reveals a cutting social satire, where the upper and lower classes are dissected, their lifestyles examined for all to see on the page, where doctors never visit the houses of the poor and maids work day in day out, cleaning the houses of the rich who, 'sleek and fat' and sitting around idly in their stately piles, are oblivious to the plight of the lower orders. From Jean de la Fontaine onwards, fables would never look back, or be quite the same again.

Part Three

Modern Fabulists and the Modern Novel

Robert Walser:
from fables to microscripts

It isn't at all surprising to find, coupled with the emergence of the modern novel, the continuing influence of Aesop's fables. It seems natural to us now, looking back, that storytelling (in all genres) and the Aesopic tradition seem to coexist naturally. Yet for many modern readers today, fables are still perceived as a children's genre that is of little intellectual significance to mature readers. On the contrary, I would argue the Aesopic fable is essential to the unique development of the novel in all its guises throughout western culture, and the reading and understanding of the Aesopic fable in relation to its burgeoning development is just as important as the perceived influence of, say, Aeschylus and Sophocles.

From Cervantes' *Don Quixote* (whose own fables have influenced many), through to the metafiction of Laurence Sterne's *The Life and Opinions of Tristram Shandy* and the fabulous lyricism of Italo Calvino's *Numbers in the Dark and Other Stories*, Aesop looms large (each of these three great novelists could command many studies of the influence of Aesop in their work alone). But I, at least, have had to make the leap from Jean de la Fontaine to where I believe the influence of Aesop starts to infiltrate modern literature in new and exciting ways: Modernism. In this section, I will concentrate on some of the Modernist novelists who have written what I would consider to be modern fables.

In *What Ever Happened to Modernism?* the novelist and critic Gabriel Josipovici suggests that Modernism deals 'not with characters or ethics but event – with something unfolding which lies beyond our immediate understanding, and certainly beyond that of the protagonists, something they are caught up in rather than the plots devised by traditional novelists.'[17] This seems to be exactly what is at play in many of the modern fables that follow. Vanished is any trace of a moral or ethical blueprint and in its place stands a continuous ripple of unfolding possibilities – a sense of event and actions. When Virginia Woolf, in her 1919 essay 'Modern Fiction'[18], called for a writer who could 'base his work on his own feeling and not upon convention, there would be no plot, no comedy, no tragedy, no love interest or catastrophe in the accepted style' she need have looked no further than Robert Walser.[19] Walser's fiction, drenched as it is in the fabulous, wore a style that hovered effortlessly above the common tropes of fiction, leaving behind formulaic, clunky and empirical characterisation for a more impressionistic feel.

Although firmly entrenched in the Modernist tradition, it is sometimes difficult to locate the writings of Robert Walser in a wider context, so deliriously self-contained and idiosyncratic they may seem to new readers. But don't allow this to put you off, if you haven't read him his writing is a wonderful odyssey of inner conflict and experimentation. Walser's sole artistic experiment was to eschew thought completely, famously declaring that he never once corrected a single line of his work. Such literary insouciance prompted Walter Benjamin to declare that 'we do not have to believe this, but would be well advised to do so. For we can set our minds at rest by realising that to write yet never correct what has been written implies both the absence of intention and the most fully considered intentionality.'[20] As Walser himself succinctly demonstrates in his novel *Jakob von Gunten* from 1909:

> To be robust means not spending time on thought but quickly and quietly entering into what has to be done. To be

wet with the rains of exertion, hard and strong from the knocks and rubs of what necessity demands. I hate such clever turns of phrase. I was intending to think of something quite different.

(Jakob von Gunten, trans. Christopher Middleton, New York Review of Books Classics, 1999)

Admired greatly by Kafka, he published short stories, verse dramas and novels regularly from 1901 to about 1929, when he suddenly admitted himself into a mental asylum, famously quipping to friends, who asked him about his writing, that he wasn't there to write but to be mad. It turned out that this had been a lie, and in fact Walser had indeed continued to write. After his death in 1956[21] numerous fragments of paper were found amongst his possessions, each covered in his handwriting. It was at first thought that these fragments and scraps were a symptom of his mental illness (they were thought to be secret codes and messages), but on closer inspection it became apparent that Walser had been writing in a minuscule *Kurrent* script (literally around 1–2 millimetres in height), an old form of German handwriting based on medieval cursive writing called *Alte Deutsche Schrift* (Old German Script) which Walser would have had to learn as a child. After much scholarly detective work, these fragments and scraps of paper were compiled, deciphered, translated and finally published together as *Microscripts*.

It is a wondrous collection of fictions, full of the familiar Walserian playfulness and fears; yet, embedded within, with added vim and finesse, was a truer sense of the fabulous, a fairy-tale-like quality that firmly displayed its roots in the Aesopic tradition, and, although it can be argued that all of his work contains such traces and echoes of Aesop, it will be the *Microscripts*, for this very reason, that I will be concentrating on in this chapter.

Walser's *Microscripts*, at first glance, seem to possess all the hallmarks of a classic fable, in the sense that they read as if they are full to the brim with meaning and moral nuances. In some ways they very well might be, but if you begin to look closer you soon realise that they are works of surface language – a surface where language is allowed to exist on its own dazzlingly brilliant terms. Take the microscript 'Swine', for example:

A person can be swinish in matters of love and might even succeed in justifying himself to a certain extent. In my opinion, various possibilities would appear to exist with regard to swinishness, etc. Someone might happen to look like a person who appears to be a swine, and all the while he is at bottom perhaps fairly upstanding. [...] If morality itself can, as it were, be a bit swinish, no one will wish to undertake to deny that it is a useful, that is, a culture-promoting swine [...] No one can claim that he is not a swine.

(Robert Walser, 'Swine', *Microscripts*, trans. Susan Bernofsky, New Directions/Christine Burgin, 2010, pp. 27–34)

The cleverness of this excerpt (written in 1928 on the back of a scrap of paper ripped from a magazine), of course, is in the simple repetition and variants of the word 'swine'. It seems to float, to hover outside and above the rest of the piece; instead of dwelling on meaning, we become enrapt in sound and amusement. What at first seems to be some moral judgement soon morphs into something quite different: a rather playful joke, mocking the serious intentions of the reader perhaps, or an exercise in authorial insouciance. Or does it? The boundaries of seriousness and playfulness are blurred and we really don't know on which side of the fence we should sit. Snappy ambiguities such as this are intrinsic to the make-up of Walser's writing, where nothing can be nailed down and pure language reigns, existing in a linguistic ether where meaning and thought are teasingly left behind. We suddenly begin to see omniscient instruction disappear; there is no need for a lesson to be learned, or for instruction to be conveyed, what we see is the emergence of a system of literature that exists within its own organic terms.

The other thing I find incredibly exciting about Walser's *Microscripts* is how similar they feel to pretty much all of the modern flash fiction published today on the internet and in literary journals (something I will discuss in Part Four, focusing on the work of Tania Hershman). The *Microscripts* feel every bit as modern and stylised as contemporary flash fiction does today.

This becomes even stranger when we begin to take into account the literal scale of this piece of writing – it is truly minuscule. As Susan Bernofsky points out in the informative introduction to her recent translations, Walser sometimes 'used the pages of tear-off calendars, cutting them in half lengthwise before filling them with text, or else the cover of a penny dreadful so its blank underside could become his tabula rasa. At the larger end of the spectrum, he once got hold of a number of sheets of the 13 x 21.5 cm paper used for art prints. On twenty-four such pages he composed a novel.'[22]

Such behaviour can seem odd to say the least. So just what was Robert Walser – as Gabriel Josipovici points out – 'caught up in' here? Why was he trying to reduce his text (creating a fable-like air to his whole oeuvre in the process)? Why reduce literature in this way? Why compress the long, descriptive, character-led passages his contemporary readers were used to reading suddenly into quirky, acid-tongued and utterly stylish snippets of prose? In a letter he wrote to his friend, the editor Max Rychner, in 1927 (two years before he was declared schizophrenic), he gives us an insight:

> [...] approximately ten years ago I began to first shyly and reverentially sketch out in pencil everything I produced, which naturally imparted a sluggishness and slowness to the writing process that assumed practically colossal proportions [...] This pencil method has great meaning for me [...] I can assure you (this all began in Berlin) I suffered

a real breakdown in my hand on account of the pen, a sort of cramp from whose clutches I slowly, laboriously freed myself by means of the pencil. A swoon, a cramp, a stupor – these are always both physical and mental. So I experienced a period of disruption that was mirrored, as it were, in my handwriting and its disintegration, and when I copied out the texts from this pencil assignment, I learned again, like a little boy, to write.

(Robert Walser, *Briefe*, ed. Jörg Schäfer with Robert Mächler, trans. Susan Bernofsky, Frankfurt am Main, 1979, p. 300)

Could the origins of the style of flash fiction we read today lie in the individual trauma of one man? Maybe, but it doesn't begin there. Walser was well-versed in the European fables of his childhood education and it seems only natural that as a man, retreating from the world, he would retreat into himself as a result (the systematic use of medieval *Kurrent* text, something he learnt as a child, also denotes this fact). In this respect, the size and stylised otherworldliness of the Aesopic fable seem like a perfect blueprint to return to for Walser – and many scholars would argue that herein lie the origins of his child-like 'pencil method'.

In any case, it was within literature that Walser found his true solace, as *'So here was a book again'* clearly demonstrates:

So here was a book again, and again I was introduced to a woman. I've acquired quite a few female acquaintances by reading, a pleasant method for expanding one's sphere of knowledge, though one can certainly, I admit, become lazy in this way. On the other hand, characters in books stand out better, I mean, more silhouettishly from one another, than do living figures, who, as they are alive and move about, tend to lack delineation. The one who is my subject here found herself, as the wife of a tradesman who trafficked in cattle, not just neglected but downright oppressed.

[...] Now, though, she began to contemplate vile and wicked things and did in fact set out one day in search of adventure, intending to become a rogue. Soon she succeeded in casting her spell on a dancer who became her admirer. [...] The woman wedded to the tradesman soon assumed the name 'the lady in green feathers'. She called to mind a vision of springtime. But sweet and dear as she looked, her thoughts were hard, and she was set on using them to debauch these insolent debauchees.

But she deceived many, turning to crime to support her extravagant tastes and lifestyle. With complete disregard for her new husband she took him down with her to the 'bottom-most level of criminality' where, after she was caught, they were both brought to trial:

> While the dancer and his colleague were sentenced to hard labor – admittedly regrettable – the blue-eyed, fabulously beautifully clothed damsel, who resembled a woefulness as she reposed within her own lovely being, found herself, on account of her justified innocence and to the joy of both herself and her defender, acquitted. When her husband heard the verdict, he too was relieved, as if he had never meant to cast her down, and now he lifted her up. Indignantly she thrust his hands away. Yet she was beholden to her lawyer, who sympathised with her. Thus does one go from happiness to unhappiness and then from unhappiness back to happiness again.
>
> (Robert Walser, 'So here was a book again', *Microscripts*,
> trans. Susan Bernofsky, New Directions / Christine Burgin, 2010, pp. 49–53)

This microscript was found written on the torn-off front cover of a penny dreadful called *After the Torment* and is said to have been inspired by its plot. It is thought Walser wrote this sometime between 1930–3, during the time he spent as a voluntary patient at the Waldau sanatorium, and it is understood that he wrote many such pieces, all of them inspired by the dramatic plots to be found in the numerous penny dreadfuls he enjoyed reading. Whenever I think about this concept, devised as it was by Walser in isolation, away from any literary or artistic avant garde, I cannot help but think of the work of contemporary postmodern artist, novelist and literary provocateur Stewart Home, whose own early novels assimilate and lift from the plot structure of pulp fiction titles from the 1970s and beyond. In Walser's writing can be found the same high jinks we today recognise in the art of Stewart Home where, just like Walser, something new and high-concept is created out of the old and the low.[23] But whereas Home reiterates and juxtaposes his assimilations via the language of literary theory, Walser reiterates his trashy plots via the tropes of fables.

The above microscript reads as fable, it possesses all the traits of language we find in fables throughout the ages – it even has its own humorous epimythium at the end. Its trickery is some feat: possessing all the weight of something literary, inscribed with meaning, something mythic even, whilst displaying origins that lie in the humble penny dreadful novels of his time. Such overt lifting and mishmashing of styles and theory was unheard of in Walser's day (the writings of his fellow Modernists had hardly broken free of Modernism's select, close-knit readership at the time he composed many of these pieces), especially something written in a medieval high-German script.

Could this solitary 'clairvoyant of the small', as W.G. Sebald later called him,[24] have simultaneously created the blueprint of both postmodern fiction and flash fiction? It's an exciting question to ask, and there's lots of fun to be had trying to answer it. I would like to think he did, somewhere in his own splicing together of fable and the penny dreadful. And if this proves to be the case – *what a remarkable feat.*

Franz Kafka:
trauma, humour and modernism

At best, as we have seen throughout their history, the average Aesopic fable can convey to the reader the deepest sense of heartfelt tragedy via a self-deprecating economy of wit and humour. Modernism, born out of a strange concoction of isolated and collective trauma,[25] easily adopted the tragicomic underpinnings of the fabulist tradition, to help galvanise a sense of foreboding and dread in keeping with – and at the same time distancing itself from – the times.

The humble fable, both in structure and imagination, was a perfect blueprint for writers such as Kafka, Walser and Svevo to use and manipulate, as it could be employed to concisely transmit a cryptic communiqué of existential alienation from the self and its being in the world, whilst simultaneously tuning in to a collective, universal set of common and recognisable mythologies.

Although there is more than a tangible scoop of crippling anxiety and angst poured into each page of his oeuvre, it cannot be denied that Franz Kafka is, on the whole, a funny writer. His work is literally brimming with humour, albeit a sense of humour that can only ever be tolerated by those possessing considerable mettle. Consider, then, David Foster Wallace's argument about 'the really central Kafka joke: that the horrific struggle to establish a human self results in a self whose humanity is inseparable from that horrific struggle. That our endless and impossible journey toward home is in fact our home.'[26] Okay, this is gallows humour and probably not to everyone's taste, but if you compare this deep-rooted sentiment with many of the Aesopic fables, such as 'The Fisherman and the Octopus', 'The Fisherman and the River' and 'Prometheus and the Two Roads', then things begin to click. What we are seeing in Kafka's work is the same urge to convey both the struggle and contradictions of existence; a collective and individual effort fraught with myriad paradoxical turns.

The short life of Franz Kafka can at times read like a fable itself, littered as it seemed to be with equal measures of tragedy and farce – most of it as surreal and haunting as that experienced by many of his own literary creations. If his diaries served to record his mental conflict and continual breakdown, then his fiction served as a respite from this; an attempt to transform all of the inner torment and failure into something unreal… something far more manageable.

Kafka published little through his lifetime; of the eleven copies of *Metamorphosis* that were sold Kafka bought ten of them. Incidentally, it is noted that Kafka became quite obsessed with this, growing increasingly paranoid over the question of just who bought it. For Kafka, the real terror was the fear that that single copy had been bought by his father. The three unfinished novels he left us with and the majority of his stories and fables existed in fragments, manuscripts and notes which were collected together by his close friend Max Brod after his death in 1924.

Reading Kafka, especially his shorter work (of which he left a lot), it becomes apparent that the Aesopic fable was a major thematic, moral and structural influence. It is no surprise, then, that Kafka's most famous fable is his most recognisably Aesopic. 'A Little Fable' uses classic Aesopic tropes to convey a sinister and uniquely Kafkaesque scenario:

'Alas' said the mouse, 'the world is growing smaller every day. At first it was so big that I was afraid, I ran on and I was glad when at last I saw walls to the left and right of me in the distance, but these long walls are closing in on each other so fast that I have already reached the end room, and there in the corner stands the trap that I am heading for.' 'You only have to change direction,' said the cat, and ate it up.

('A Little Fable', *The Great Wall of China and other short works*, trans. Malcolm Pasley, Penguin Modern Classics, 2002, p. 135)

Immediately, we are in familiar Kafkaesque territory, a terrain where the 'world is getting smaller every day'. It's not just a momentary observation; it is something that is felt each new day. And even when the world was bigger it still invoked fear. Existence is maze-like, full of walled corridors leading us to a place we do not want to go, evoking a sense of unanswerable dread, a threatening landscape of confusion and inevitability. A particular modern trait that Kafka introduces to the development of the Aesopic fable, and, in turn, of Modernist literature, is his use of geometry (we only have to read the work of contemporary novelists such as Jean-Philippe Toussaint and Tom McCarthy to understand just how far his influence has travelled). Within the structure of 'A Little Fable' the geometry of the 'horizon/mousetrap' dichotomy is at play. It is a purely spatial fable in which we begin to see the mouse's horizon shrink from view and the walls around it begin to close in, creating a claustrophobic snare, blocking the mouse from ever reaching the horizon. Like any mouse caught in a trap, Kafka's is shown to the reader as an innocent victim, one that is permanently trapped. For Kafka's mouse, space and distance suddenly shortens and the geometry of its world changes, strangulating its existence. The geometry of its world (represented in both matter and metaphor), soon becomes the sole embodiment of the entire fable. For Kafka, the horizon is finite in distance and this distance must somehow be completed alone. Yet Kafka's mouse cannot be alone: perpetually caught in a world of terrifying dimensions, in the 'end room' of its short life lies the cat, craftily changing the direction of the lone mouse, devouring it before the already disappearing horizon is reached. Kafka's geometry creates an astonishing paradox: we are stuck in an ever-changing environment, populated with magnificent vistas that can never be reached. I can't help but think it is this very paradox that both terrified and amused Kafka throughout his life.

In this short space of time we feel the obfuscation and terror that Kafka is trying to convey. Yet, at the end, we laugh. There is a great sense of humour at play here. It is a sense of humour that is steeped in dread and anguish. After the rather tortuous journey of life – where you are free to make your own choices, but seldom ever do – there is nothing at the end of it but the cruel snare of death itself:

'You only have to change direction,' said the cat, and ate it up.

Kafka's humour lies in this line: 'You only have to change direction.' He knows, the mouse knows, the cat knows and the reader knows: we're never going to make that one simple little change and even if we wanted to we are pretty much powerless to change it.

There are further echoes of this humour in the fable 'The Departure':

I ordered my horse to be fetched from the stable. The servant did not understand me. I went into the stable myself, saddled my horse, and mounted. In the distance I heard the sound of a trumpet; I asked him what that meant. He knew nothing and had heard nothing. At the gate he stopped me and asked: 'Where are you riding to, master?' 'I don't know,' I said. 'Just away from here, just away from here. On and on away from here, that's the only way I can reach my goal.' 'So you know your goal?' he asked. 'Yes,' I replied, 'I've just told you. Away-from-here – that is my goal.' 'You have no provisions with you,' he said. 'I need none,' said I, 'the journey is so long that I must die of starvation if I get nothing on the way. No provisions can save me. It is, fortunately enough, a truly immense journey.'

('The Departure', *The Great Wall of China and other short works*, trans. Malcolm Pasley, Penguin Modern Classics, 2002, p. 137)

Yet again we are thrown into a world steeped in confusion, where simple instructions are not understood and sounds which cannot be heard resound across a vast landscape without meaning. Kafka's world is one of deep misunderstanding and crippling fear – all born out of the trauma of existence: to merely exist is enough, more than enough to fuel the desire to escape the here and now. And again, Kafka's humour kicks in the moment we realise there is nowhere to escape to, that no matter how far we travel, we will be forever bound by the shackles of existence.

We are beginning to see the fable, through Kafka's adaptation of the Aesopic tradition, find new ground via a thoroughly modern context. In fact, it can be argued that Kafka single-handedly modernised the popular fable (allowing novelists such as Thomas Bernhard to exploit its influence even further), injecting into its structure the recognisable tropes that seem to be synonymous with modern existence: deep-felt alienation, the mechanisation of society and the drone-like existence of the populace (especially those in menial jobs). Disappeared from the modern fable, then, is much of the anthropomorphism, gone are the animals and in their place are everyday people: workers, servants, police officers, et cetera. Gone is any apparent moral implication and in its place is inserted a deep-rooted honesty and acceptance, not of defeat, but of uncertainty, one which is repeated ad infinitum: there is no place to go, there is nothing new to learn, yet still we must go on, still we must complete life's journey – even if this journey leads to nothing but ruination and suffering:

All the suffering around us must be suffered by us as well. We do not all have one body, but we all have one way of growing, and this leads us through all anguish, whether in this or in that form. Just as the child develops through all life's stages right up to old age and death (and basically each stage seems inaccessible to the previous one, whether longed for or feared), so also do we develop (no less deeply bound up with mankind than with ourselves) through all the sufferings of this world. There is no room for justice in this context, but neither is there any room for fear of suffering or for the interpretation of suffering as merit.

('The Collected Aphorisms, 102', *The Great Wall of China and other short works*, trans. Malcolm Pasley, Penguin Modern Classics, 2002, p. 97)

Kafka introduces the reader to a certain sense of *knowing*. A seen-it-all-before style of fable, where modern readers are cryptically acknowledged as being far too long in the tooth to swallow well-worn didactics, yet still in tune with the struggle of suffering Kafka is trying to convey. Take 'On Parables', for example:

There were many who complained that the words of the wise are always mere parables, and of no use in daily life, which is the only life that we have. When the wise man says: 'Go across', he does not mean that one should cross over to the other side of the street, which is at least something that one could manage if the result were worth the effort; he means some fabulous yonder, something that is unknown to us and that even he cannot designate more precisely, and therefore something that cannot help us down here in the very least. All these parables mean really no more than that the inconceivable is inconceivable, and that we knew already. But the cares that we actually have to struggle with each day are a different matter.

One man then said: 'Why do you resist? If you followed the parables, then you would become parables yourselves, and thus free of your daily cares.'

Another said: 'I bet that is also a parable.'

The first said: 'You have won.'

The second said: 'But unfortunately only in parable.'

The first said: 'No, in reality; in parable you have lost.'

('On Parables', *The Great Wall of China and other short works*, trans. Malcolm Pasley, Penguin Modern Classics, 2002, p. 184)

Kafka, whilst mocking the 'words of the wise' as 'mere parables' which are not much 'use' in modern, everyday society, has fun using the very same construct to illustrate his point. What we predominantly witness in 'On Parables' is a wonderfully tricksy meta-fable, which dissects the fable's usage in modern society. He points us towards some 'fabulous yonder' where the everyday can still be analysed and reinterpreted – whilst still maintaining the feel of the fabulous[27] – and even if each fable or parable means 'really no more than that the inconceivable is inconceivable, and that we knew already' it can still be used to convey the everyday speech of modernity. It is this sense of *already knowing* that Kafka cleverly brings to the genre – the same self-awareness that is now widely used within postmodern iterations of the everyday and the fabulous in art, literature, music and modern culture.

Throughout all art, whether it be self-conscious or not, Kafka points us back towards the everyday struggle of existence; some-thing which art cannot erase, never fully releasing us from our 'daily cares'; even within the 'fabulous yonder' of art, reality intervenes and the struggle continues.[28] Through art the strug-gle becomes more visible, something Kafka illustrates through-out his work as our inability to accept the same *suffering*.

Nearly all of Kafka's writing is concerned with this struggle, and whereas his longer fictions collectively strive to *become the struggle* itself, his shorter work continues in its *knowing*, creating a haunting distance from the work. 'A Comment' is a wonderful example of such foreboding, albeit infused with the humour of self-awareness:

It was very early in the morning, the streets were clean and deserted, I was going to the station. As I compared my watch with the clock on a tower I saw that it was much later than I had thought, I had to make great haste; in my alarm at this discovery I became unsure of the way, I was still something of a stranger in this town; luckily there was a policeman at hand, I ran up to him and breathlessly asked him the way. He smiled and said: 'Do you expect to discover the way from me?' 'Yes,' I said, 'since I cannot find it myself.' 'Give it up, give it up,' said he, and he turned away with a great flourish, like a man who wants to be alone with his laughter.

('A Comment', *The Great Wall of China and other short works*, trans. Malcolm Pasley, Penguin Modern Classics, 2002, p. 183)

As well as being a funny and quirky tale this short fable, especially when considered alongside the rest of his shorter work, marvellously warns us against seeking escape from existence – in true Kafkaesque fashion we do not know what this escape might be, we are simply presented with a figure who has to get somewhere, in this case to the station. Kafka uses the policeman at night to signify omniscient authority, a figure we naively put our trust in (and, incidentally, is commonly used in early Modernist fictions as a symbol that is both menacing and humorous – the policeman scene in Knut Hamsun's *Hunger*[29] is a notable example). We suddenly become as shocked as the man himself when the policeman exclaims: 'Do you expect to discover the way from me?' From here on in the man is left standing, there is no escape, he – like us – must accept existence and the struggle of suffering; there is no escape from the anguish and trauma it causes. As nihilistic and depressing as this may seem, this is not something to fear, nor is it something to be used self-righteously, in pure Kafkaesque fashion this is simply something which we must endure – in many ways pointing us towards Aphorism 103:

You can hold yourself back from the sufferings of the world, that is something you are free to do and it accords with your nature, but perhaps this very holding back is the one suffering that you could avoid.

('The Collected Aphorisms, 103', *The Great Wall of China and other short works*, trans. Malcolm Pasley, Penguin Modern Classics, 2002, p. 97)

Kafka's fables are infused with the same sense of dread and trauma that is recognisable throughout his entire oeuvre, but unlike his longer fictions, they are on the whole far more playful, displaying his unmistakable sense of humour to its fullest potential. And although each is steeped in the same anxiety we immediately recognise as Kafkaesque, they also manage to reflect a lightness of touch, whilst still being as dark and foreboding as can be.

In exploring this playfulness, through the Aesopic tradition, Kafka has single-handedly paved the way for the modern fabulists I will be discussing in Part Four. Kafka facilitated, through his modern fables, a sense of absurdity that can easily be recognised and understood by modern readers – deceiving us along the way with a macabre sense of humour.

James Joyce: 'In the buginning is the woid'[30]

If Jean de la Fontaine's fables guide his contemporary readers towards the possibilities of his chosen genre, then James Joyce's rewriting of Jean de la Fontaine's 'The Ant and the Grasshopper' in *Finnegans Wake* demonstrates just how far the Aesopic fable can be (and was) stretched, morphed and completely reorganised into another system of linguistic being and meaning.

Joyce's beguiling 'The Ondt and the Gracehoper', the second fable included in *Finnegans Wake* after the equally beguiling 'Mooske and the Gripes',[31] is not only my favourite rewriting of an Aesopic fable, but is also evidence of the genre's infinite possibilities predicted by La Fontaine. Its genesis for Joyce lies in the eternal Shem / Shaun polarity that haunts *Finnegans Wake* – Joyce's 'Ondt' and 'Gracehoper' represent the two elements of this polarity. In fact, Joyce's fable – as it becomes his own – serves as an exploration of, as we shall see, pretty much anything he wanted. But it became famous (as did *Finnegans Wake* itself) for his quarrel with Wyndham Lewis.

To focus on this most magnificent of literary spats just for a moment: the row in question stems from Lewis' review of *Ulysses*[32], in which he condemns Joyce's novel as 'material that was scraped together into a big, variegated heap', adding 'I regard *Ulysses* as a time-book; and by that I mean that it lays its emphasis upon, for choice manipulates, and in a doctrinaire manner, the self-conscious time-sense, that has now been erected into a universal philosophy' and concluding that 'at the end of a long reading of *Ulysses* you feel that it is the very nightmare of the naturalistic method that you have been experiencing.' Joyce, upon reading this review, set out to write the record straight, re-drafting many sections of *Finnegans Wake* in direct response to Lewis' review, culminating at his most confrontational in his fable 'The Ondt and the Gracehoper'. 'Ondt' (Danish, meaning 'Evil' and also close to the English 'Don't') is clearly not only meant to be Shaun, but Lewis himself ('a well-tall fellow, raumybult and abelboobied'[33]), while the music-making and famished 'Gracehoper' (more than a nod and a wink to Joyce's own story 'Grace'[34]) is both Shem and Joyce ('blind as a batflea'[35]). As in La Fontaine's rewriting, as well as the Aesopic original ('The Ant and the Dung Beetle'[36]), themes of time and space are observed, but in Joyce's version the question of time and space does not go unresolved. Joyce seeks to unravel their complexities within the scope of literature.

Joyce's fable was composed in March 1928 and is used by many Joycean scholars as the key to unravelling both the Shem/Shaun polarity and Joyce's own thoughts on space and time in relation to Wyndham Lewis' critique. It begins after Shem asks Shaun for a song:

> — So vi et! we responded. Song! Shaun, song! Have mood! Hold forth!
> — I apologise, Shaun began, but I would rather spinooze you one from the grimm gests of Jacko and Esaup, fable one, fable too.
>
> (*Finnegans Wake*, Penguin Books, 1992 edn, p. 414)

Shaun, flatly fusing to sing, an art he finds purely temporal, considers the fable of 'The Ondt and the Gracehoper'. The 'Ondt' (=Shaun=Lewis) keeps food and money stored away over summer, so that in winter he has food aplenty:

who, not being a sommerfool, was thothfolly making chilly
spaces at hisphex affront of the icinglass of his windhame,
which was cold antitopically Nixnixundnix

(Finnegans Wake, Penguin Books, 1992 edn, p. 415)

Unlike the 'Gracehoper' (=Shem=Joyce) who spends the summer singing and thinking about art:

Now whim the sillybilly of a Gracehoper had jingled
through a jungle of love and debts and jangled through a
jumble of life in doubts afterworse

(Finnegans Wake, Penguin Books, 1992 edn, p. 417)

Come wintertime, when the Gracehoper, hungry and poor, asks
the Ondt for money he flatly refuses. So the Gracehoper finally
sings his song as a riposte, blaming the Ondt in the process.
Joyce's fable, in its entirety, is more than impressive: it is a work
of sonorous, etymological, entomological, critical and linguistic
wonder, whorling between a discourse on Schopenhauer, Kant,
Berkeley, *The Egyptian Book of the Dead* and Indian philosophy to
a Darwinian exercise in biology and entomology, then tackling a
multifarious unification of space and time via Einstein, whilst
elucidating the complexities of temporal and musical structures
within the nature of existence, all wrapped up in a thunderously
cryptic and hilarious debunking of Wyndham Lewis' proclama-
tions. Its scope is, indeed, epic.

The Aesopic motif of time and space within this fable is ever-
present, especially the passing of time and space and their separation, concluding in a rather Joycean (albeit via Einstein)
coming together of their parts cast through the prism of
chimera. As a visual allusion to space and time itself Joyce uses
Schopenhauer ('Schoppinhour'[37]) himself as a signifier:

He would of curse melissciously, by his fore feelhers, flex-
ors, contractors, depressors and extensors, lamely, harry

me, marry me, bury me, bind me, till she was puce for
shame and also fourmish her in Spinner's housery at the
earthsblest schoppinhour so summery as his cottage, which
was called fourmillierly Tingsomingenting, groped up.

(*Finnegans Wake*, Penguin Books, 1992 edn. p. 414)

Schopenhauer rethought the whole world as some kind of grand
idea in our imagination – or, as he called it, our 'visibility of
will'.[38] It seems that Joyce concurs with this premise (not only
for the purpose of his fable, but for *Finnegans Wake* as a whole,
referencing Sanskrit leitmotifs which help to posit the same prin-
ciples in the veil of Maya,[39] for example). Joyce is attempting to
unravel this premise with his fable: centred round a reflection of
things that resemble nothing else – everything is pure allusion –
thus dispelling Lewis' own preoccupations with space and time
elsewhere.

'Tingsomingenting' in Danish means 'a thing like no thing',
brilliantly shoehorned into this section just to help hammer
home his point. Or, as Samuel Beckett liked to describe *Finnegans
Wake*, it is 'not *about* something: *it is that something itself*'.[40] I
guess the fun lies in trying to catch the *thing* – whatever that *thing*
may be. Joyce's common idea is to unite any conflicting sources
– to help establish a unity of thought and space: *Finnegans Wake*
is essentially a retelling of the world as it appears, represented in
waves of language, veiled and ciphered in layered façades (think
radio waves, frequencies we have to tune in to in order to hear
and understand more clearly). It is a world in which things stay
the same and only change in their retelling; a world part void, or
as Joyce would have it, a 'woid' – this is Joyce retelling the representation of our never-changing, never-ending world through
the ever-changing, always-beginning veil of the fable, in the hope
that his retelling will unveil things as they are and show us that
things, although pretty much *no-thing*, are essentially the same
thing. Joyce loved such contradictions and relished inflicting
them upon his readers. Fables reflect life without the aid of

realism, or concrete foundation; they are as much governed by myth as they are by language – and herein, for Joyce, lay their power. 'The Ondt and the Gracehoper' is Joyce's grand announcement, his unveiling that serves to dispel not only Wyndham Lewis' own conceits, but our own philosophically governed world of separation and free will – a world in which, through time, we struggle to gain a foothold, whorling within the void of its being.

In bringing spatial and temporal realms together, Joyce points the reader towards their universal opposition, both surpassing Newton's laws and debunking Lewis' own musings. Like Einstein, Joyce has unified time and space, but has also revealed their constant juxtaposition. Such a contradiction (and *Finnegans Wake* is constructed around them) serves to argue that nothing is fixed or indeed separated and everything begins and ends in the same origin, or as Joyce (inspired by Giambattista Vico[41]) liked to put it 'by a commodius vicus of recirculation'[42] (or even: 'harry me, marry me, bury me').

The spat between James Joyce and Wyndham Lewis is now legendary and firmly lodged within literary/Modernist folklore. In *Time and Western Man* (of which 'An Analysis of the Mind of James Joyce' appears in chapter XVI) Lewis announces his polemic on the new 'time school' writers such as Woolf, Proust, Faulkner, Stein, Mann and Joyce himself, all influenced by the philosophies of Henri Bergson.[43] The book is a scathing, ironic attack, written in a venomous tone, probably adopted by Lewis in response to his contemporaries' rejection of his somewhat 'over-ambitious' proposed project to steer Modernism towards the 'revolutionary action' he thought it should strive for. Whereas Joyce aimed for a unification of time and space, Lewis called for their separation, revelling in their contradictions as a mode for creative energies. For Lewis, Space was everything: it generated stability, classicism and the rise of individual consciousness, whereas Time stood for everything he believed ruined art's progress: change, the collective consciousness and romanticism. In what can only be described as a personal tirade against Joyce, Lewis accuses him of 'shabbiness' and likens *Ulysses* to an 'all-life-in-a-day-scheme' which compressed the present out of all recognition. Such accusations must have hurt Joyce, and indeed they did as *Finnegans Wake* is littered with allusions and references to their spat: *Time and Western Man* becomes 'Spice and Westend Woman'[44] in *Finnegans Wake*, and Wyndham Lewis is constantly referred to as 'wind hound loose'.[45]

In Joyce's fable, Lewis is sided with the space-orientated Shaun, as opposed to the temporally obsessed Shem. Lewis as 'Ondt' is a spatial entity, rather 'chairmanlooking when not making spaces in his psyche'.[46] The temporal 'Gracehoper', although he does not have the upper hand in the fable's long history, is orchestrated by Joyce to have the last word, in a wonderful fable-as-promythium / endomythium / epimythium-all-rolled-into-one scenario.

> The thing pleased him andt, and andt,
> He larved ond he larved on he merd such a nauses
> The Gracehoper feared he would mixplace his fauces.
> I forgive you, grondt Ondt, said the Gracehoper, weeping,
> For their sukes of the sakes you are safe in whose keeping.
> (*Finnegans Wake*, Penguin Books, 1992 ed., p. 418)

The song begins with the outright pleading (*pleased*) of don't (*andt*) before the familiar insect motifs infest and plague each of the following lines of the song. We see numerous references to laughing and larvae (*larved*) juxtaposed with sickness, noise and nausea (*nauses*). The Gracehoper continues:

> I pick up your reproof, the horsegift of a friend,
> For the prize of your save is the price of my spend.
> Can castwhores pulladeftkiss if oldpollocks forsake 'em
> Or Culex feel etchy if Pulex don't wake him?
> (*Finnegans Wake*, Penguin Books, 1992 ed., p. 418)

Is Ondt=Lewis looking a gifthorse in the mouth (*horsegift*) in his damning attack on time? Or has Gracehoper=Joyce wasted the gift of time itself? The following vitriol gives us a clue as to just where Joyce's sympathies lie. The theme of twinning appears in the myth of Castor and Pollux mixed with filth and outrage (*castwhores pulladeftkiss*), where gnats and arses (Latin *Culex*: gnats and French *Cul*: arse) mix with bollocks and fleas (latin *Pulex*: flea).

What is at first striking about this spellbinding song, apart from its sonorous qualities, is the spatiotemporal interplays between past, future and present, where characters, historical figures and insects collide without boundaries:

> A locus to loue, a term it t'embarrass
> These twain are the twins that tick *Homo Vulgaris*.
> (*Finnegans Wake*, Penguin Books, 1992 ed., p. 418)

In these two lines alone we can see references to locusts (*locus*), ticks (*tick*) and termites (*term it*), alongside references both to place (Latin *locus*: a place) and time (*term*), the oxymoronic twins (*twain/ twin*) which should be embraced (*t'embarrass*), though they also embarrass the likes of Lewis, by the common man (*Homo Vulgaris*) – which in turn is a reference to Lewis' *Time and Western Man*.

More importantly for any reader, Joyce's own exploration of temporality and music is to be found in this fable; unlike the earlier fable of 'The Mooske and the Gripes', this time Joyce leaves nothing unresolved. To bring more spice to his riposte, Joyce galvanises his intentions further:

> An extense must impull, an elapse must elopes,
> Of my tectucs takestock, tinktact, and ail's weal;
> (*Finnegans Wake*, Penguin Books, 1992 ed., p. 418)

Here Joyce makes explicit his tactics (*tectus*) in these lines (in the way only *Finnegans Wake* can), putting a secure roof (*tectus*: Latin *tectum*: a roof) on the notion that although space (*extense*) and time (*elapse*) must obey the laws that govern one another, they must also act as one together, orchestrating (*takestock*: German *Taktstock*: baton) their union. Joyce ends this song, in an unforgettable and direct reference to Lewis (which I believe, incidentally, to be the single most brilliant and cutting critique in literary history), with these wonderful and infamous parting lines:

> Your feats are enormous, your volumes immense,
> (May the Graces I hoped for sing your Ondtship song sense!),
> Your genus is worldwide, your spacest sublime!
> But, Holy Saltmartin, why can't you beat time?
> (*Finnegans Wake*, Penguin Books, 1992 ed., p. 419)

In 1929 the literary journal *Transition*, edited by Joyce's friend Eugene Jolas, asked its readers/writers to sign a petition titled 'The Revolution of the Word Proclamation' referring to a manifesto that appeared in issue 16/17. Both Jolas' short introduction and provisions 2, 4, 10 and 11 are of particular interest when seen in relation to Joyce's usage of fable to denounce Lewis' own failure to write a time-school novel:

> Tired of the spectacle of short stories, novels, poems and plays still under the hegemony of the banal word, monotonous syntax, static psychology, descriptive naturalism, and desirous of crystallizing a viewpoint...
>
> 2. THE IMAGINATION IN SEARCH OF A FABULOUS WORLD IS AUTONOMOUS AND UNCONFINED.
> (*Prudence is a rich, ugly old maid courted by Incapacity...*
> *Blake*)

4. NARRATIVE IS NOT MERE ANECDOTE, BUT
THE PROJECTION OF A METAMORPHOSIS OF
REALITY.
(*Enough! Or Too Much!... Blake*)

10. TIME IS A TYRANNY TO BE ABOLISHED.

11. THE WRITER EXPRESSES. HE DOES NOT
COMMUNICATE.

('The Revolution of the Word Proclamation', *Transition*, Issue 16/17, 1929)

Although Joyce didn't sign the petition there is no doubt that it was in his mind during the composition of 'The Ondt and the Gracehoper'. And certainly *Finnegans Wake* fitted Eugene Jolas' own ideas of how the novel should and could beat the classic notions of time that governed literature at that period (and still do to this day). Through his fable Joyce manages to combine day-time and night-time into one continuous dream-time that singularly spans *all time* and refutes its omnipotent presence. *Finnegans Wake* encompasses the historical and the everyday, together with the fantastic and the primal (all becoming one and the same, in a narrative outside and within time), becomes a collective consciousness of event and imagination. It leaves the reader breathless in its damnation of time and posits the question: if James Joyce could beat time, why couldn't Wyndham Lewis?

Finnegans Wake is a complex mechanism designed and assembled bit by bit in a series of careful additions to systematically abolish the interference of classic notions of Time in the modern novel, via an amalgamation of world history, language and myth. In resurrecting this assertion through an allusion to the fables of Aesop, the bugs and insects associated with *The Egyptian Book of the Dead*, and the Irish ballad of Tim Finnegan (Joyce takes his title from this ballad, after many attempts; a tale of a man resurrected from the dead at his own wake), Joyce has unlocked the true undying potential of all literature, in which time plays no part. 'In the Buginning is the woid',[47] or in the beginning the story becomes void, which is a combination of the beginning and the end all rolled into one. A recirculation that defeats time; both reflecting the circular structure of *Finnegans Wake* and the notion that, unlike time, all myth and fable is without beginning or end.

Jorge Luis Borges:
the illusion of reality

Much has been written about how little Jorge Luis Borges wrote, it can even be argued that he was more of a reader than a writer, but it is impossible to simply ignore the influence of his work, stretching far and wide as it does, openly acknowledging his debt to myth and fable along the way – so it comes as no surprise that I have included his work in this brief history. The short fables written by Borges are glorious things, almost bursting at the seams with knowledge and themes of endless recurrence, the circular repetition of world history (think both Joyce and Nietzsche), motifs of the dream within the dream (Shakespeare) and the hallucinatory re-imagining of the world/universe (Schopenhauer) – and all of this in nothing more than a few collections of fables and short fiction.

In fact, his entire oeuvre is a series of fictions (or *ficciones* as he liked to call them) of the fantastic and the hyperbolic; ironic in tone, they openly discard the wish-fulfilment promise that litters much literature of a similar ilk. His work serves to block any inspirational pathways. It is a collection of fictions that continually turns in on itself, always revealing its own peculiar brand of invention; critiquing itself in the process, as it tightens until firmly locked in a perfect vacuum of its own creation.

Borges has always been explicit in his intentions, stating in his own epilogue to *Other Inquisitions*, a collection of his philosophical essays, that 'the quantity of fables or metaphors of which man's imagination is capable is limited, but that this small number of inventions can be everything to everyone.'[48] Probably the finest elucidation of this limitedness in Borges' fictions appears within 'Pierre Menard, Author of the Quixote', a wonderful piece of writing in which the eponymous author sets himself the task of rewriting Cervantes' *Don Quixote*, not as some literary or artistic interpretation, but rather as a literal rewriting of the entire text *word for word*. The crux of this fiction, and of Borges' own theoretical *world-literary-mythological* overview, is staggering:

> The text of Cervantes and that of Menard are verbally identical, but the second is almost infinitely richer.
>
> ('Pierre Menard, Author of the Quixote', *Labyrinths*, trans. James E. Irby, Penguin Classics, 2000)

And, in both insouciance and seriousness in equal measure:

> It is a revelation to compare Menard's *Don Quixote* with Cervantes'. The latter, for example, wrote (Part One, Chapter Nine):

> … truth, whose mother is history, rival of time, depository of deeds, witness of the past, exemplar and adviser to the present, and the future's counsellor.

> Written in the seventeenth century, written by the 'lay genius' Cervantes, this enumeration is a mere rhetorical praise of history. Menard, on the other, writes:

> … truth, whose mother is history, rival of time, depository of deeds, witness of the past, exemplar and adviser to the present, and the future's counsellor.

> History, the *Mother* of truth: the idea is astounding. Menard, a contemporary of William James, does not define history as an

inquiry into reality but as its origin. Historical truth, for him is not what has happened; it is what we judge to have happened.

('Pierre Menard, Author of the Quixote', *Labyrinths*, trans. James E. Irby, Penguin Classics, 2000)

For Borges this simply translates as: the text we read is not necessarily the text of the author – i.e., the *Don Quixote* we read is not necessarily that of Cervantes. Each new author simply rewrites the masterpieces of old, nothing is original, but everything is new – in this sense, Borges argues Menard's *Don Quixote* is just as, if not more, valid than Cervantes'. And why shouldn't it be? We simply rewrite the mythologies of old, to create new mythologies. Everything, for Borges, is mythology and a blurring of illusion and reality. James E. Irby argues that 'Borges's fictions, like the enormous fiction of *Don Quixote*, grow out of the deep confrontation of literature and life which is not only the central problem of all literature but also that of all human experience: the problem of illusion and reality.'[49] It is a dichotomy that is easily accommodated by the humble fable, where the blurring of illusion and reality can find a safe home. Borges entertains this marvellous dichotomy in his wondrous 'The Parable of Cervantes and the Quixote':

Tired of his Spanish land, an older soldier of the king sought solace in the vast geographies of Ariosto, in that valley of the moon where the time wasted by dreams is contained, and in the golden idol of Mohammed stolen by Montalbán.

In gentle mockery of himself, he imagined a credulous man who, perturbed by his reading of marvels, decided to seek prowess and enchantment in prosaic places called El Tobosco or Montiel.

Vanquished by reality, by Spain, Don Quixote died in his native village in the year 1614. He was survived but a short time by Miguel de Cervantes.

For both of them, for the dreamer and the dreamed one, the whole scheme of the work consisted in the opposition of two worlds: the unreal world of the books of chivalry, the ordinary everyday world of the seventeenth century.

They did not suspect that the years would finally smooth away that discord, they did not suspect that La Mancha and Montiel and the knight's lean figure would be, for posterity, no less poetic than the episodes of Sinbad or the vast geographies of Ariosto.

For in the beginning of literature is the myth, and in the end as well.

('The Parable of Cervantes and the *Quixote*', *Labyrinths*, trans. James E. Irby, Penguin Classics, 2000, p. 278)

This passage ends in, for me, probably the single most succinct summation of what literature is and always has been: myth-making; a blurring of the everyday with the unreal. As circular and infinite as this may at first seem, there is also a fragmentation of the real at play here; what we are seeing is the novel (in this case Cervantes') critique itself for not really succeeding, unable as it is to capture the reality of the everyday. Borges' short fable points this out, arguing that the writing of reality is in itself a form of myth-making – and just like the fables of old, there is an element of the unreal in which we invest our own realities as we read.

The other one, the one called Borges, is the one things happen to. I walk through the streets of Buenos Aires and stop for a moment, perhaps mechanically now, to look at the arch of an entrance hall and the grillwork on the gate; I know of Borges from the mail and see his name on a list of professors or in a biographical dictionary.

('Borges and I', *Labyrinths*, trans. James E. Irby, Penguin Classics, 2000, pp. 282–3)

Borges is the same Borges who like 'the other one' shares a fondness for 'hourglasses, maps, eighteenth century typography, the taste of coffee and the prose of Stevenson' but 'in a vain way that turns them into the attributes of an actor'. Like Samuel Beckett, and poets such as Wallace Stevens, Borges is expressing the expression of an imagination that is witnessing its own death. Put simply, the imagination becomes something possessed by another imagination; something at the far reaches of a shared reality which is, rather ironically, the closest thing to us (or, in Borges' case, Borges himself):

> Little by little, I am giving over everything to him, though I am quite aware of his perverse custom of falsifying and magnifying things. Spinoza knew that all things long to persist in their being; the stone eternally wants to be a stone and the tiger a tiger. I shall remain in Borges, not in myself (if it is true that I am someone), but I recognize myself less in his books than in many others or in the laborious strumming of a guitar.
>
> ('Borges and I', *Labyrinths*, trans. James E. Irby, Penguin Classics, 2000, pp. 282–3)

Borges ends this beguiling parable in a fabulous haunting of the self:

> Thus my life is a flight and I lose everything and everything belongs to oblivion, or to him.
>
> I do not know which of us has written this page.
>
> ('Borges and I', *Labyrinths*, trans. James E. Irby, Penguin Classics, 2000, pp. 282–3)

Here we subtly witness the fable imploding; the author is questioning the very existence and nature of the text we are reading. Whereas, in the past, we took fables to mean something – something we could take away with us, something to improve our lives – now we begin to see a fable that audaciously calls such meaning into question, arguing that the fable (and, in fact, all of literature), being part of a vast tradition, must be allowed to exist on its own terms 'because what is good belongs to no one, not even to him [the author of the fable], but rather to language and to tradition'.

Even the everyday fables we write aren't our own; they belong to something other, where language and myth converge – in this sense, both reader and author are merely onlookers, each tuning in to a bigger picture. All literature can be contrived, allowing the literature we create to justify us – even when we aren't sure who has written it, interwoven as it is with what has already been. With this in mind what at first glance looks like an obstacle, soon begins to show us the true possibilities of literature.

Borges argued, in light of such perceived fragmentation and separation from everyday reality, that all fantastic literature exists within a fourfold structure, beginning with 'the work within the work, the contamination of reality by dream, the voyage in time and the double.'[50] With this in mind, it is Borges' own trick to insert these new realities into our mind, without obfuscation and overt tomfoolery, by simply acknowledging the merging of the everyday world with myth and the world of the reader – for Borges, this must always be a seamless process, as it is for him one and the same. He achieves this by acknowledging his sources, because nothing is original, everything is a translation of a 'pre-existing archetype'[51], and with this the trick is seamless because we, the readers, have already seen it before, even though we hardly recognise it. Literary insouciance and trickery like this takes great skill and intelligence to pull off. But if we accept it for what it is, what is there to be fearful of? Our narratives are merely the stuff of fable and mythology.

In perhaps one of his most telling fables, 'Everything and Nothing', Borges ties together mythic elements with the stuff of dream, existence and a sense that we are acting within the realm of a fabulous dreamt reality (the classic dream-within-a-dream scenario common to many modern fables). It is probably the most fitting place to leave Borges, before we move on first to Thomas Bernhard, who in 104 short stories made Borges' assertion of inauthenticity in art tangible, and then to a group of contemporary writers (in Part Four), who have turned the unreality of reality and existence on its head, creating their very own metafictional role-play of 'Everything and Nothing' in their wake:

There was no one in him; behind his face (which even through the bad paintings of those times resembles no other) and his words, which were copious, fantastic and stormy, there was only a bit of coldness, a dream dreamt by no one. At first he thought that all people were like him, but the astonishment of a friend to whom he had begun to speak of this emptiness showed him his error and made him feel always that an individual should not differ in outward appearance. [...] At the age of twenty-odd years he went to London. Instinctively he had already become proficient in the habit of simulating that he was someone, so that others would not discover his condition as no one; in London he found the profession to which he was predestined, that of the actor, who on a stage plays at being another before a gathering of people who play at taking him for that other person. His histrionic task brought him a singular satisfaction, perhaps the first he had ever known; but once the last verse had been acclaimed and the last dead man withdrawn from the stage, the hated flavour of unreality returned to him. He ceased to be Ferrex or Tamberlane and became no one again. Thus hounded, he took to imagining other heroes and other tragic fables. And so, while his flesh fulfilled its destiny as flesh in the taverns and brothels of London, the soul that inhabited him was Caesar, who disregards the augur's admonition, and Juliet, who abhors the lark, and Macbeth, who converses on the plain with the witches who are also Fates. No one has ever been so many men as this man who like the Egyptian Proteus could exhaust all the guises of reality. [...] For twenty years he persisted in that controlled hallucination, but one morning he was suddenly gripped by the tedium and the terror of being so many kings who die by the sword and so many suffering lovers who converge, diverge and melodiously expire. [...] He had to be someone; he was a retired impresario who had made his fortune and concerned himself with loans, lawsuits and petty usury. [...] History adds that before or after dying he found himself in the presence of God and told him: 'I who have been so many men in vain want to be one and myself.' The voice of the Lord answered from a whirlwind: 'Neither am I anyone; I have dreamt the world as you dreamt your work, my Shakespeare, and among the forms in my dream are you, who like myself are many and no one.'

('Everything and Nothing', *Labyrinths*, trans. James E. Irby, Penguin Classics, 2000, pp. 282–3)

Thomas Bernhard:
rewriting the everyday

If Kafka's sense of the everyday in the modern fable was one
of an ever-shrinking landscape and geometry, irrevocably woven
in dark humour and trauma, then Thomas Bernhard's 104 short
stories, which make up the whole of *The Voice Imitator*,[52] serve as
a canny reversal of this personalised use of space and emotion.
As Bernhard's work clearly demonstrates, the mythology of the
everyday is not only something which perpetually folds in on
itself, as Kafka and Borges pointed out, but something which
spirals outwards, both startlingly and repetitively, in vitriolic
obsessions and acerbic expansions of voice, communication and
unsentimental documentation – a recurring form of extraordinary reportage.

In these 104 stories, Bernhard tackles the everyday by rewriting it. Like Borges, in doing so he transforms the everyday into
a dizzying and fabulous mythology; a collection of fables that
also works as a mini-anthology of Bernhard's own political,
emotional, intellectual and artistic obsessions, taking in 'one
love affair, thirteen instances of lunacy, four disappearances,
twenty-six murders, two instances of libel, six painful deaths,
three character attacks, five early deaths, one memory lapse,
four cover-ups and eight suicides'.[53] Each of these stories is taken
from, or made to read like, an everyday event, or observation.
Bernhard was an avid reader of newspaper articles and many
of the stories are direct rewritings of what he had read. In one

sense, each story is a real event, in another it is transformed into a recognisable mythology, a fantastic event which speaks for all of life's absurdities . . . it is modern fable taken back to its satirical Aesopic roots without aping its traditional tropes.

Like the original Aesopic fables, Bernhard's stories (some barely a page long) are satirical and scathing retakes of actual events – although, as we begin to see in all modern fabulists, there is no sign of a moral subtext at play. In its place is a continuation of Kafka's *knowing*, only instead of being used to signpost us to what we already know, it is used to hoodwink us, to pull the rug from under our sophisticated feet. Bernhard uses his reportage of the everyday to highlight the complex failure of language to capture everyday life's absurdities, revealing in a flash (rather than a twist) that such reportage only serves to add to life's absurdity. For example, Bernhard marvels in the flash of sadness turning to humour when rewriting the horrific consequences of the death of a young boy in a house fire:

> A woman in Atzbach was murdered by her husband because, in his opinion, she had carried the wrong child with her to safety from their burning house. She had not saved their eight-year-old son, for whom the man had special plans, but had saved their daughter, who was not loved by the husband. When the husband was asked, in the District Court in Wels, what plans he had had for his son, who had been completely consumed in the fire, the husband replied that he had intended him to be an anarchist and a mass murderer of dictatorships and thus a destroyer of the state.
>
> ('Unfulfilled Wish', *The Voice Imitator*, trans. Kenneth J. Northcott, University of Chicago Press, 1997, p. 71)

Bernhard takes the same humour we see displayed in Kafka's writing to a whole new level. In rewriting familiar, everyday reportage, Bernhard highlights the paradox in such practice:

the simple, highly entertaining fact that it always reads as fiction – in a sense mythologising itself. Readers, and I include myself in this group, recoil at the absurdity of such events, instantly calling into question the legitimacy of the story. Bernhard, instead of empirically documenting his rewriting fact by fact, or by inserting the flowery tropes of literature to mask it in beauty, simply turns the story into a fable, by allowing the narrative that already exists to do its own work, further highlighting its astonishing absurdity, but also cataloguing a mythology of untrue *truisms* in the process. With this sneaky turn of events in mind, where truth is turned *unbelievably* true, I challenge any reader not to laugh out loud whilst being moved by the deep-felt trauma experienced by the humble postman in 'Madness':

A postman was suspended in Lend because for years he had not delivered any letter that he thought contained sad news or, in the nature of things, any of the cards announcing a death that came his way, but had burned them all in his own home. The post office finally had him committed to the lunatic asylum in Scherrnberg, where he goes around in a postman's uniform and continually delivers letters that are deposited by the asylum's administration in a letter box specially built into one of the walls of the asylum and that are addressed to his fellow patients. According to reports, the postman asked for his uniform as soon as he was committed to the lunatic asylum in Scherrnberg *so as not to be driven mad*.

('Madness', *The Voice Imitator*, trans. Kenneth J. Northcott, University of Chicago Press, 1997, p. 96)

This is classic Bernhardian satire with an acid kick – something that his novels and plays are littered with, driving not only him, as author, forward, but dragging the reader with him to wherever he wants to take us. There is no sympathy for us or his subject, just a need to show in his rewriting the unique absurdity of the everyday. And oh my, how funny is this, how scandalous to mock a supposedly true story. But what are we laughing at? Are we laughing at the postman, the real postman? Or are we laughing along with Bernhard? I would suggest neither; in fact, I would argue that we are laughing at ourselves, at our own naivety, the shame of being hoodwinked by the author (and no doubt he is laughing at us also) into a sense of false security. All the while Bernhard is simply pointing out that everything is fiction, even the short, snappy reportage of the everyday. This is the ultimate, all-encompassing fable, a trick that involves everyone and everything; the everyday, like literature itself, is pure mythology. As the French critic and theorist Maurice Blanchot states in his essay 'Everyday Speech', 'the everyday is no longer the average, statistically established existence of a given society at a given moment; it is a category, a utopia and an idea, without which one would not know how to get at either the hidden present, or the desirable future of manifest beings.'[54] The sense of the everyday that Bernhard rewrites as reportage is never an 'average' account of a 'society at a given moment', it is instead a 'category' of events, observations and happenings, that when combined serve as an idea by which the everyday is reinvented into something that alerts its readers towards a present so near and ordinary it becomes 'hidden' by this very premise – thus, we invent a new reality from it. Bernhard's stories, his fables, unlock the possibility of fictionalised public space and its outward trajectory, which in turn unravels the 'future of manifest being': a form of fantastical repetition. In other words, in creating a myth out of our hidden present, a present of newspaper clippings, breaking news stories, events and observations, Bernhard reveals to us the true potential of our collective and everyday being: a truth/untruth dichotomy, based on the repetitive public narratives of our present. Yet, even this isn't enough to galvanise our position, as Maurice Blanchot goes on to explain that 'whatever its other aspects, the everyday has this essential trait: it allows no hold. It escapes. It belongs to insignificance, and the insignificant is without truth, without reality, without secret, but perhaps also the site of all possible signification. The everyday escapes. This makes its strangeness – the familiar showing itself (but already dispersing) in the guise of the astonishing.'[55] Bernhard never lets go of the same 'essential trait' that Blanchot posits, his 104 stories hang in the ether; neither true nor false, a mythology of insignificant untruths, that are made all the more astonishing in their significance and truth.

Such truth/untruths, however, are seldom seen by each and every reader they meet. In 'Beautiful View', a story at odds with the majority of the collection in that it takes place out in the wilderness rather than in an urban centre, Bernhard posits this very same question, this time using a newspaper story about the death of an eminent professor to illustrate this:

On the Großglockner after a climb of several hours, two professors, close friends, from the University of Göttingen, who had been staying in Heiligenstadt, had reached the spot in front of the telescope which is mounted above the glacier. Skeptics though they were, they could not fail to be impressed by the unique beauty of the mountains, as they had constantly assured one another, and when they arrived at the spot where the telescope was mounted, one of them kept asking the other to be the first to look through the telescope, so as to avoid being reproached by the other for pushing himself forward in order to look through the telescope first. Finally they agreed that the older and more cultivated and, in the nature of things, the more courteous should take the first look through the telescope, and he was overcome by what he saw. However, when his colleague approached the telescope, he had hardly put his eye to it when he gave a shrill cry and dropped dead. To this day, the friend of the man who died in this remarkable way still wonders, in the nature of things, what his colleague *actually* saw in the telescope, for he certainly did not see *the same thing*.

('Beautiful View', *The Voice Imitator*, trans. Kenneth J. Northcott, University of Chicago Press, 1997, p. 20)

Bernhard understands that all fiction is open to interpretation. What one reader might see in a text another might not – everything within the rewriting of the everyday is weighed down by this paradox: we never know what is being told or heard, we can only give our own interpretation of what is brought forth via the text; as in all events, each is governed by its own mediation. It is how we, as readers, respond to its mediation that counts. We often 'wonder' ourselves, just like the professor, what it is others actually see through the telescope, the lens of interpretation and mediation, for we rarely see 'the same thing'.

Aesop's own fables were orchestrated to show and tell, to convey a collective morality and understanding: we were all expected to see the same thing. Whereas now we see the modern fable metamorphosed into its very own entity: something different yet immediately recognisable, a fragmented whole, distant in its closeness, a code without rule, escaping everyday repetition via its own repetitions, always ready for interpretation, an event without cause forever waiting to be used. We're not meant to see the same things any more, as Gilles Deleuze once reminded us, alerting us to the fact that 'we live today in the age of partial objects, bricks that have been shattered to bits, and leftovers. We no longer believe in the myth of the existence of fragments that, like pieces of an antique statue, are merely waiting for the last one to be turned up, so that they may all be glued back together to create a unity that is precisely the same as the original unity.'[56] Indeed, things have certainly moved on.

In 'Two Notes' Bernhard purposely splits and fragments one of his own stories by shoehorning in his own supposed interpretation (albeit one of feeling):

In the large reading room of the Saltzburg University
Library, the librarian hanged himself from the large chan-
delier because, as he wrote in a suicide note, after twenty-
two years of service he could no longer bear to reshelve
and lend out books that were only written for the sake of
wreaking havoc, and this, he said, applied to every book
that had ever been written. This reminded me of my grandfather's brother who was the huntsman in charge of the
forest district of Altentann near Hennsdorf and who shot
himself on the summit of the Zifanken because he could no
longer bear human misery. He too left this insight of his in
a note.

('Two Notes', *The Voice Imitator*, trans. Kenneth J. Northcott, University
of Chicago Press, 1997, p. 64)

As readers we can pretty much read anything we want into
the first half of this cleverly assembled story. Yet, surprisingly,
Bernhard pinpoints it to a particular event, something personal
to him, a gut-wrenching moment of poignancy. With this in
mind we still can detect some distance, as Bernhard is only
'reminded' of an event from the dusty annals of his own family's
history, something which had happened not to his father, or
his grandfather, but to his 'grandfather's brother' – a link to a
family fable, maybe? Most definitely a story passed down (probably orally) through the immediate generations, and now boldly
cemented, firmly within the realms of the fabulous and the
astonishing, in print. We cannot really argue with Bernhard's
usage and understanding of the power and lineage of fable in
modern literature here, linking as he so effortlessly does the
fabulous stories of the everyday with the inherently personal and
heartfelt. It's a wondrous touch. To which I can't help but think,
have we been hoodwinked yet again?

In this blurring of fact and fiction Bernhard catapults the fable
outwards in all directions, delivering to us an insight into the
pain and absurdity of modern existence, revealing in the process

his own heartfelt desire to catalogue it. Fables used in this way are quietly devastating, given their ironic tone and ability to hoodwink the reader; in the way that when reading newspaper clippings, their imagery and power remain within us: quietly, yet with considerable precision. It is a modern, journalistic voice injected into an old Aesopic tradition, purposely harking back to the first iterations of Aesop: the ability to convey the deepest of human emotions with satirical dexterity and the keen eye of a sniper, picking off unsuspecting targets one by one.

Although Bernhard's view is one of deepest cynicism, it has to be acknowledged that he has played his part in bringing the fable back to the everyday (essentially transporting it back to readers of modern literature), by unearthing the fact that it has never really gone away. It has been with us all the time; it's just been too close for us to see it. Bernhard achieves this by grounding fable in modern events, via a system of mediation that is instantly recognisable to us: the newspaper article, the arena in which the modern fable is published every day. It is, then, no real coincidence that the majority of Bernhard's 104 stories take place in urban centres away from the more traditional environments of the fable (the earth, forest and sea, for example). Bernhard's fables take place where newspapers are printed and sold; in the streets of towns and cities. It is a wonderful turn of events which sublimely echoes Henri Lefebvre's own views that 'the street tears from obscurity what is hidden, publishes what happens elsewhere, in secret; it deforms it, but inserts it in the social text.'[57] If this isn't a perfect summation of the machinations at play in each and every one of Bernhard's 104 stories, I don't know what is. It is every bit the 'Everyday Speech' of Blanchot. Bernhard's reportage lives within the everyday, in which the everyday is 'anyone, anyone whatsoever, who does so, and this any-one is, properly speaking, neither he, nor, properly speaking, the other; he is neither the one nor the other, and he is the one and the other in their interchangeable presence'.[58] The everyday, then, is published under its own terms, away from the inability of language, expressing itself within a 'medium which alienation, fetishisms, reifications produce their effects'.[59] These 'effects' being, in Bernhard's case at least, a rewriting of the everyday in which his stories become this process manifest.

For me, Bernhard's stories, as fabulous as they undoubtedly are (and I mean this in its original etymological context), unearth probably art's dirtiest secret: that art, *all of art*, isn't authentic, it is purposely taken from the everyday, a series of iterations reiterating one another; a grand reportage of what has already been, happening again and again.[60] This may very well be the most fabulous thing, not only about Thomas Bernhard's collections of everyday fables, but everyday art also.

Part Four

Post-Fabulists, Meta-Fabulists and Flash Fiction

Blake Butler:
dismantling ordinary things

As I mentioned in the introduction, I have tried to discuss the influence of the Aesopic fable, as I see it, within the unique architecture of modern literature and the novel. As you can see, I have only scaled the tip of a very large iceberg (to say the least), such is the wondrous diversity and wealth of world history contained in the writing of what we know as mere fables. The aim of this brief history is to bring the fable to a modern context, a plateau which we can categorise as modern.

In exploration of the diverse group of writers that follow, I feel each will convey their own unique and idiosyncratic take on the Aesopic tradition and its history and influence in their writing. From the experimental and dizzying fragmentation of Blake Butler, to the wonderfully concise flash fiction of Tania Hershman, we will begin to see how the humble fable is still dazzlingly adapted within new and exciting avenues of modern literature's development.

As Borges quite rightly said, 'every writer creates his own precursors. His work modifies our conception of the past, as it will modify the future.'[61] I would like to argue that the writers whom I discuss next (especially Blake Butler and Shane Jones) owe in their own particular brand of literature and interpretation, a large debt to the writing discussed in Parts One, Two and Three. Again, this is a subjective group and in no way a full and precise representation of the contemporary writers who fit this mould (had this book been larger, I could easily have included chapters on established novelists' work such as Robert Coover's mesmerising collection *Pricksongs and Descants*, Jonathan Lethem's anthropomorphic *Chronic City*, J. Robert Lennon's ruminative *Pieces for the Left Hand*, Marie Darrieussecq's mesmerising *Pig Tales*, and any of the novels of Jean-Philippe Toussaint, whose works all possess the same Aesopic influences, and more recently the middlebrow works of Téa Obreht and Helen Oyeymi). I feel that each contains a uniquely modern feel, whilst still maintaining the fabulous, other-worldly elements to be found in the Aesopic tradition. I also wanted to discuss a group of writers who are on the cusp of creating a new generation of writing; a group of writers from whom I feel there is much more to come.

This chapter will concentrate on Blake Butler's debut novella *Ever* (he has since published another novella, *Scorch Atlas,* and a novel, *There Is No Year*). Put simply, Blake Butler's fictions make the ordinary visible in fantastic ways. *Ever* is every bit a work of fiction of Beckettian significance, in both its layering of feeling, place and time, and its pared-down, yet beautifully crafted prose. In this context its literary permutations are quite staggering, yet the book is such a flimsy little thing in comparison, contradicting contemporary American novelists' preference for writing large, analytical texts that can also serve as pretty decent doorstops. *Ever* posits a peculiar scenario: body in room. In fact, it is a room within many rooms; a house turning and folding into many more, a multi-layered fiction of space and time, feeling and memory, light and dark. Butler exemplifies this by surrounding his text in multiple parentheses, both signifying the beginning and ending of one space, or room, with another, whilst lending the text a sense of its own limitlessness whorling within a space of its own creation:

[There are thirteen plastic doors in this house, and I have been through none. None have hinges, handles, or keyholes. Only some have knobs.

[Sometimes when I am careful I hear people talk through certain of the doors.]]

(*Ever*, Calamari Press, Nairobi/Detroit, 2009, p. 14)

Immediately we are gripped by a sense of confusion and terror; this is an hallucinatory world filled with paranoia and uncertainty, but a world that is instantly recognisable to the reader: a house, doors, people, hinges, handles and keyholes. It is a world of upturned reality, this all may seem real, but the actions and perceptions contained within each parenthesis are wholly astonishing, gripped as they are in the fabulous world of its own contradictory making:

[The only door I ever went through was in the crawlspace under the den. It was unlocked and came right open. Behind the door, there was a light. There was a corridor. The air was cool. There weren't any other doors or pictures. It went on and on.

[The door beside my front door confuses me when I am tired.]

[There are several large bumps beneath my hair.]]

(*Ever*, Calamari Press, Nairobi/Detroit, 2009, p. 21)

In this paradoxically closed world, confusion and uncertainty rules action, even the thought of another door and what lies behind it is filled with both nothingness and endless possibilities. As in the fictions of Borges, Joyce or Beckett, *Ever* is a novella that exists both outside and inside the parameters of time and space, where past and future unite to form one unanswerable moment after another, where nothing can be represented as we see things within ourselves, behind the light of our eyes looking out. For

Butler, this is a fictionalised space and time firmly rooted in the real, an *Ever*-present, governed by the possibility of a ubiquitous light, that is discoverable outside reality. Its echoes and rumblings of unanswerable representation parallel Beckett's own sense of *empêchement*[62], or the struggle for rapprochement with the objects of the narrator's conscious mind, where objects become un-representable because they simply are what they are. Butler's narrator reads as a Beckettian 'skullscape'[63]; a mind's eye representing both a *self* and *unself*, looking out, observing the light beyond the pane from within. The multitudinous rooms of the house, in this respect, serve as a repetitive mirroring of the narrator's mind struggling to cope with what it simply sees, both aware and unaware that the language it uses in the process is forever useless and unknowable: there is no house, there are no doors, no female 'I', just a series of words stumbling and unfolding as they fail to describe the light of being through feeling:

[The thing about the moving, then, inside the other house is this: there I begin to feel alive. I mean coming through the door even that first time, I felt eruption in my hair. I felt an ocean, or something liquid, flushing through the insides of my skin, around my abdomen or womb. A gush or warming throb. I would admit to sensual elaborations but I can't be sure that this was that. As you know or may have heard there are often not the words for sorts of things in which you feel as if something about you is not the same, or if it might be in the midst of shifting, or. The floor in the hallway inside the front door was dark and made of wood. It had a seamless finish. *See?* I could slither on it. I could be. The hall's walls were also seamless and hung with photos of faceless men. By faceless I mean their fronts were facing backwards, away from the camera, from me. It was not certain what they'd been made to look at, what they wanted, who they'd need.

[No one came to see.]]]

(*Ever*, Calamari Press, Nairobi/Detroit, 2009, p. 33)

Butler's narrator is forever stuck in the process of trying to express what cannot be expressed, forced to recognise that 'there are often not the words for sorts of things'. She becomes a camera; a lens looking out, never fully understanding what there is to look at. As readers, we counter the narrator's ontological responses to such impossibilities, with her dreamt possibilities: the opening, un-opening of doors, the taste of light and surface invoking memory and feeling, the feel of space closing in on itself, the forming of mind maps of an ever-present life contained within the surface of things – these things being the fabulous uncertainties of place, history and time. In this respect, *Ever* reads as a fable unfolding and revealing the ordinary things we take for granted, the things ordinary reality stops us from seeing. It is only when the real is mythologised in this way that we truly begin to see the real:

[I dreamt there was a door inside my stomach. It was gray and had a curtained window. I could feel the doorbell on my tongue.

[Some nights in bed I'll lay with my face pressed against the door lodged in my headboard and I will hold my breath and I will listen.

[Other nights I sleep.]]]

(*Ever*, Calamari Press, Nairobi/Detroit, 2009, p. 22)

Within this space is also the sense of repetition, where words constantly repeat themselves and begin to sound unfamiliar to the narrator. Within these repetitions the narrator begins to question the authenticity of each word spoken, finding within each question a sense of inner dislocation, both from what is spoken and from what is seen. Within the cacophony of repetition and language we are given a feeling of the narrator spiralling into the mythology of her own creation: a form of sullied, second-hand language that that gives birth to untranslatable myth:

[When that prayer was over I began again.

[When that prayer was over I began again.

[When that prayer was over I began again.]

[I hadn't meant to speak in repetition; and yet did so out of something in me wanting. By the fifth instance the words slurred slightly, skewed from my original intention ~ and yet I did not pause or cause correction. I spoke into the room and felt it fill. My voice sounded only slightly off. Some scrunched foundation in me, gonging. The itch ripped in my throat. My spit came up in long black strands. Susurration in my vision. I touched my throat bulb. The thing was thrumming. I spoke an awful language. I heard myself confess to things I had not done.

[I told myself to find the door.]

[I moved towards the door that held the outside, where I could taste the air the way it was ~ *wart and charcoal and skin powder* ~ but as I neared the door ~ *not me moving but something moving me* ~ I began to feel heavy and more tired, more dumb and dumb and dumb ~ *inflating* ~ until at one point, short of exit, I found myself curled on the floor, cramped and breathing harder than I'd ever,

so hard I couldn't see ~ *not that I'd want to or that*
it mattered ~ so hard I felt my teeth would jar out
and open, skunked with guggle.]]]

[I could see the door still a little.

  [I could ~ still could ~ see the door.

    [Door (s)(s).

      [Def.: *door* (n): 1. a thing I'd noticed.

        [2. A thing through once I'd ~

          [once I'd ~ been.]]]]]]]

(*Ever*, Calamari Press, Nairobi/Detroit, 2009, pp. 25–6)

This is the underpinning dynamics of the traditional Aesopic
fable (an everyday reality reconstructed into another world), in
this case transformed into anamorphic processing: the layering
and distorting of one form of language and image into another;
where a distillation of both poetics and mythology transforms
the familiar into something other-worldly, a code of visual
fictions, each repeating the simple linguistic, phonic and optic
building blocks of the everyday. Vision is interrupted by soft
'susurrations' to create an audible event on the page, and language once spoken becomes something unrecognisable – almost
disowned. Butler's narrator is dismembering the everyday, bit by
bit, through language, vision and sound, and rebuilding it into
a fable of ordinary events lost in a vortex of misunderstanding
and misinterpretation. We begin to see what is missed, as time
slowly descends into something of no consequence and the
everyday actions of the narrator are relayed back to us in a form
of mythic slow motion. The door, a thing stripped to a mere

noun, is something that is seen by the narrator, and the movement towards it is heavy, though 'not me moving but something moving me'. We witness her ontological struggle with the nature of each interpretation, played back to her in the confusing, dream-like fictional construct of space and environment, at a speed that feels heavy and forced. Through this distillation into slow motion, made up of the language and things she sees and hears (and in turn begins to find impossible to translate) we begin to invent the world around her, *for her*. Forgetting that what we are reading is a series of words spiralling within the darkness looking out. What is this door? What lies behind it? Where is this house? Whose house is this? In stripping back language, through repetition, to sound, touch and vision Butler has reopened our horizons and we read this fiction through the mythic, where the possibilities of its actions are endless. Forgetting, in the process, that what we are seeing is what we already know; the ordinary everydayness of a room in a house.

The original impulse contained within *Ever* is mythic. It is the first thought, before language, like Aesop's first impulse: to simply *tell*, when he was given the gift of speech. Then comes the light behind the eyes; or the light beyond the pane, or lens of looking; then comes the body with all of its visceral functionalities and parasitical traits: menstruation, secretions, skin as caul or sack; the body as a host for all manner of mould, fungi and bacteria. Butler charts the object realistically as a fully functioning organism, taking us back to a process that acts before humanistic traits of language and back to matter, before form and beauty (the flowery and ironically unrealistic tropes of modern literature) to a space of original impulse. In tracing the roots of this antediluvian impulse in *Ever* back to the same Aesopic desire to communicate what is seen with the gift of speech, we begin to see from where our own desire to be moved by fables stems: the same unknowable desire to *tell*, to attempt to fathom the unknowable.

Just as the fables of Aesop alert the reader (via their extra-ordinary otherworldliness) to the obvious, yet hidden things of the everyday (the very things which make us tick and govern our moral actions), Butler introduces the reader to the obvious by magnifying it on the page, facilitating in us the choice to stick around and explore, or simply to be carried away by it, while never seeking himself to infuse within the text a moral code. In Butler's universe we are perpetually stuck in a world of the familiar that we do not recognise. In transforming the ordinary (rooms, houses, windows, doors and our habitation amongst these things) through language and feeling Butler creates his own, unique fable: one of touch and sense, feeling and obfuscation, language and beauty, always self-contained and self-perpetuating in a fixed, ever-present loop. Either way, just as in the multitudinous interpretations of Aesop, the experience is manifold.

HP Tinker:
jump-cuts, portholes and metafictions

HP Tinker's work is about as far removed from an Aesopic fable as one can imagine, yet it still contains the same heady mixture of the fabulous and the surreal. His collection of what I would call post-fabulist metafictions, *The Swank Bisexual Wine Bar of Modernity*[64] is a heady intersection of metafictional mischief and garrulous intellect. After reading his work, the world around us – a series of interpolations, bifurcations, jump-cuts and portholes to the symbolic and literary order, if HP Tinker is to be believed – begins to take on a whole new complexion. Unlike the pared-down language of Blake Butler, HP Tinker allows as much as possible to filter into his writing, and his influences are wide-ranging, from Paul Gauguin via Tina Turner, Jacques Derrida, Thomas Pynchon, Dean Martin and Sammy Davis Jr to Morrissey, creating a series of fictions that explain their own unique purpose as they are written. Even if we just read some of the titles of his stories recently published in *Ambit*[65], we start to see a clearer picture of just where HP Tinker's imagination lies: 'Son of Sinbad', 'Winter Kills Love Among Other Things', 'The Dead Palace', 'At The End of the Hellenic Period', 'The Fall of Bohemia', 'The Modernist Uprising' and 'Alice in Time & Space and Various Major Cities'. Indeed it's a grand symphony of intertextuality, tomfoolery and theoretical intent. For example, in 'The Minimalist', HP Tinker explains his theorem via a snappy, one line footnote (serving as an epimythium) at the end:

I went to see a minimalist. My life was complicated at the time and in urgent need of simplification. So I looked in the phone book for the number of a good one. 'Minimalism changed my life,' the minimalist said. 'Now it can change yours.'

The minimalist sat in a shiny chair, concocting grand sentences. The minimalist said my life was poorly constructed, told me to cut unwanted arrangements, unnecessary transactions, to aim for greater structure in all things. I wrote down everything the minimalist said. 'Structure brings clarity –' the minimalist explained on my thirteenth visit. '– will you be paying by Visa?' I applied the minimalist's instructions to my life, discarded what I could: ornaments, possessions, furniture, pets, friends, casual lovers. Life was simpler, but didn't feel as agreeable as it used to. I returned to the minimalist with a list of questions.

The minimalist waved them away waspishly.

'Why are you being so waspish?' I asked. The minimalist coughed awkwardly. 'Would you join me for dinner?' asked the minimalist. The minimalist took me to dinner. Afterwards, we went dancing. Afterwards, we had sex in my apartment. Afterwards, the minimalist said, 'I love you', and went home. Afterwards, the minimalist didn't phone.

* * *

I went to see the minimalist again.

The minimalist wasn't in. I phoned the minimalist. 'Please leave a message,' said the voice of the minimalist. I left several, of varying tone and content. The minimalist never called back. A week later, I broke into the minimalist's apartment. I was shocked at what I found: an abundance of neo-baroque furnishings exuding the Old World grandeur of a redesigned Budapest café; mint-green and brass interiors, stained-glass windows, gold mirrors, marble floors, flickering gothic lanterns, glittering crystal chandeliers...[1]

1. It was then I realised the minimalist was full of crap.

(*The Swank Bisexual Wine Bar of Modernity*, Social Disease Books, 2007, pp. 83–4)

There are so many ways to read this short piece. At first it reads as a simply hilarious and quirky tale, an oddity of observational skill; yet, there are obviously some deeper ripples forming underneath its surface. For instance, is HP Tinker alerting us to the absurdities of modern living? Connecting to our deep-felt need for random connections that have no real bearing on everyday life? Or is he poking fun at our many faux-pretensions, caught in a world devoid of artistic expression, a clinical modernity that hides a dirty secret? That everything is really a sham? Most probably, I feel, HP Tinker is outlining his own take on literature (and his clue lies in his perfectly executed epimythium): an all-encompassing blueprint of humour and literary pastiche, absorbing everything as he creates; being more of an assimilator of literary culture, than a writer who prefers to subtract it from any creative equation.

Somewhere caught deep within all of this is HP Tinker's own unique brand of Mancunian humour, where everyone and everything is a sitting target. HP Tinker is humorous whatever his subject, whether it be Jacques Derrida in 'The Death of the Author':

Comment Attributed To Jacques Derrida In Retrospect:

'The service was beautiful and faintly disturbing at the same time. Strikingly similar in timbre to the sad final blow of losing a relative. There was not a palpable sense of tragedy as such. Rather it felt more like the passing of a very elderly system which had done its best in the circumstances and now didn't quite work properly and so needed to be thoroughly rethought and replaced. Although virtually impossible not to be moved by the size or the spectacle or the emotion of the occasion, somehow I managed not to be. But the day was about more than the author and the death of the author. It was about bringing people together. Even Julian Barnes and Jeanette Winterson are now on speaking terms. They're planning to meet up and discuss their differences at Selfridges over potted shrimps, Dover sole, and rhubarb tart...' (© Jacques Derrida, 2003)

('The Death of the Author', *The Swank Bisexual Wine Bar of Modernity*, Social Disease Books, 2007, p. 101)

Or even Paul Gauguin in 'Paul Gauguin Trapped on the 37th Floor':

Alone in bed with his scotch, Paul Gauguin remembers his childhood with deep affection. 'My mother and older brother were highly active in the artistic struggle. One day, a group of neo-realists came for them and aggressively ransacked the house. When a tall blonde classicist asked me where they were hiding, I told him at once without hesitation. They were imprisoned for over two months in a seaside holiday camp because of my impetuosity. They tried hard, but they could never look me in the eye after that...'

Paul Gauguin has many regrets.

('Paul Gauguin Trapped On The 37th Floor', *The Swank Bisexual Wine Bar of Modernity*, Social Disease Books, 2007, p. 7)

When we read the above – which can only be described as quintessential HP Tinker – what we recognise is an open admittance of high and low culture as one and the same thing. There are no hierarchies in his metafictions. Everything is possible within one and the same system of language, where myth,

144

literary history and theory mix, opening with deadpan humour and satire. HP Tinker is candidly aware of Aesopic tropes, the use of the fantastic and the astonishing, administering his own brand of promythium, endomythium and epimythium, scattered liberally throughout the text:

The Solution Of Life's Fundamental Problems

'Could not dreams be applied to the solution of life's more fundamental problems?' Thomas Pynchon is pondering at the plinth, almost to himself, on my return. Death hangs in the air like an enormous light bulb. The general feeling amongst the congregation seems to be that Thomas Pynchon has now 'outstayed his welcome'.

('The Death of the Author'. *The Swank Bisexual Wine Bar of Modernity.*
Social Disease Books, 2007, p. 108)

From here on in Thomas Pynchon is cut from the remainder of 'The Death of the Author'. It is both funny and brutal; it is also quite telling. Pynchon is a sizable influence on the writings of HP Tinker – is he trying to exorcise Pynchon's ghost from his own text? Whatever he's doing here, it's got to be said that he's having lots of fun with it: posing a question, answering it, and then dismissing it all in the space of a few wonderful lines. Yet, what is this dream HP Tinker talks about? He's obviously referring to the work of Thomas Pynchon here, who could ever understand the gravitas of a phrase like 'death hangs in the air' without ever having read the first sentence of *Gravity's Rainbow*, for instance? But I don't think this is HP Tinker's point. I think that, like Pynchon, he sees the whole of literature as some form of dream, where time, space, locality, history and future all merge into one strange dreamtime-narrative, relayed back to us in fabular snippets of text.

I would argue that HP Tinker's writing displays many of the hallmarks of the Aesopic tradition, but it is in his fable-like story

'The Dead Palace' where he openly acknowledges this debt (in the only way HP Tinker can, that is). It begins simply:

> Today, much like yesterday, the palace lies silent at 3am, stagnant, emptied of life.
>
> ('The Dead Palace'. *Ambit*. Autumn 2005, (182):19–28)

It is an ordinary beginning, much like any other fiction. There may be a clue in the word 'palace' that something extraordinary is about to transpire, but that's about it. From here on in though, HP Tinker has the reader in the palm of his hand, we are hooked, and we are willing to be taken wherever he wants to take us. As the very next paragraph in the story demonstrates:

> At the rear of the palace in a small office reeking of mahogany sits Don Diego, former court dwarf, the floor around him scattered with many important leather bound tomes: books, scrolls, parchments, paperbacks, film guides, celebrity biographies. For fifteen years he faithfully supplied the Queen with family entertainment, general mirth, toilet humour, risotto, sexual favours, fine wine, pasta, slapstick, occasional aubergines... finding some small notoriety among the revolutionary courts of South America for his piercing good looks and experimental bedroom technique.
>
> ('The Dead Palace'. *Ambit*. Autumn 2005, (182):19–28)

The whole scene seems drenched in the fabular tone of fairy tale, yet there is something else happening, something quite modern and abrupt. 'Parchments' sit next to 'celebrity biographies, a 'former court dwarf' has become a celebrity himself in 'the revolutionary courts of South America' for no other reason than 'his piercing good looks and experimental bedroom technique'.

Not only is 'The Dead Palace' a master-class in comic writing, it also displays a cavernous knowledge of fable, myth and fairy tale, turning the common tropes of these genres upside down in the process of the unfolding story. In what soon becomes part François Rabelais[66] part Benjamin Tabart[67], 'The Dead Palace' soon falls into metafictional freefall, and HP Tinker splices many images together, encapsulating the imagery of common fable and fairy tale genres in one hilarious narrative:

> Through a forest of ill-feeling, across the blistering ice and snow of a broken heartland, up along the high ridges of the mountains of rectitude, Don Diego encounters a friendly giant, a human lobster, an evil genius, a Welsh dragon, a Cuban superstar, a cunning gnome, a French-faced damsel, a weeping camel, a bisexual siren, a veget-arian King, an oil scientist, an androgynous sailor…
>
> 'Hello,' says Don Diego, nervously.
>
> 'Oh *hi!*' says the androgynous sailor.
>
> ('Tinker, HP. *The Dead Palace. Ambit.* Autumn 2005; (182):19–28)

What we are beginning to see emerge in writers such as HP Tinker is a re-evaluation of common Aesopic tropes; those same extraordinary tales we take for granted and dismiss as child-like oddities are starting to be reclaimed, rewritten and re-used in new and exciting ways. HP Tinker is willing to take risks, morphing his fictions into other genres, stealing from others, jump-cutting to other styles and reclaiming them as his own in a post-fabulist splicing of intertextuality and *détourne-ment* where we witness the blurring of literary boundaries, many of them hijacked and forced to perform in multitudinous ways, or in a modern context, and in keeping with HP Tinker's oeuvre up-to-date, 'turning expressions of the Capitalist system against itself'.[68] Many would mistake such insouciance as care-less and ignorant, but it displays a thorough knowledge of the complexities involved in transcribing myth, fable and fantasy into workable, and ultimately readable and entertaining narra-tives.

HP Tinker is able to create a mesmerising narrative that not only takes the reader off into far distant lands, but also remains true to our sense of the everyday, lending his text a credible leverage for interpretation. What's refreshing about this is that it displays the very same techniques employed by Aesop: the ability to both transform and inform. Isn't this the crux of every fable?

Joseph Young:
from microscripts to microfictions

If there is, dare I suggest, a modern voice to whom W.G. Sebald's astute summation 'clairvoyant of the small' could easily be applied, other than Robert Walser, then it has to be the little known author Joseph Young (little-known outside of the US contemporary independent publishing and art fraternities, at least). A writer on art and collaborator with artists amongst other things, Young is part of a group of writers, mostly US-based, who are far more interested in the possibilities of a single word than the possibilities of entire novels. For Young (and I would also throw Blake Butler and Shane Jones into this particular mix), the juxtaposition of a word with another within the confines of a small sentence structure is paramount. It is a form of writing suited both to the internet (Young edits the marvellous microfiction blog *verysmalldogs.blogspot.com*) and the traditional printed book. Minuscule in form and construction, it is a fiction that needs to be devoured slowly, demanding our participation, as attention to linguistic detail – its off-beat metre, rhythm and phonemic juxtapositions – is essential to its understanding and enjoyment.

Such detail can be found in his collection *Easter Rabbit*, a series of microfictions separated into three sections, *Easter Rabbit, Deep Falls* and *God Not Otherwise*, combining a total of eighty-six microfictions some of which total as few as seventeen words. Young's microfictions often contain, in their taut linguistic construction, a haunting, abrupt discourse between one and another, part A and part B, often pronoun 'she' or 'he' in humanist-realist terms, or where noun sits strangely askew next to noun and adjective creating a coded language of extraordinary juxtapositions. Although there is an obvious narrative arc threaded through *Easter Rabbit*, I would still like to argue that these microfictions are not a form of lyrical humanism, or realism, but rather a laconic echo of *mytho-linguistic* associations, a strange form of looping back to language and its origins in the discourse and communication of myth. There are certain themes that loop within and throughout the collection, such as common themes of time, death and loss. There are also religious signifiers (the Ark, Cardinals, Eden, et cetera) which sit next to those of love and violence (the constant communication between 'she' and 'he' and the repetition of the colour red is prominent throughout, for instance), and the ubiquitous presence of water that trickles throughout the collection, offering to the reader a sense of necessity, though also echoing Young's own thoughts that microfictions should at once be both dense and transparent,[69] blends effortlessly into the three sections. Each of Young's microfictions, the smallest of fables, acts as a pair of tweezers pinpointing the minutiae of our ordinary lives, then picking them up for us to inspect. Language is manipulated by Young through a process of crystallisation until it hardens into an unbreakable and beautiful thing; something that can be inspected as a whole or, on a meta-level, observed through the microscope of our own imagination. Words, and the readers' exploration of their meaning and particular placement, are paramount. In 'Some Things Stand For Things', for instance, we can't help but wonder what, or whom the signifier or indeed the signified is. Is it the man? The boy? Or the threat of something nefarious?

The wind clung to him, his arms trailing strings of it as it blew. Across the narrow meadow was a man, one eye blackened out, the other rolling. The man gestured to him to come, that there was an opening in the hill. I can't, he shouted. It's too far. The man shook himself and spat. He'd known the type, these boys who would smother in the sun before taking a hand.

(*Easter Rabbit*, Publishing Genius Press, 2009, p. 10)

Or is it something else? The 'strings' of wind? The 'blackened out' eye? The 'smother' of sun's rays even? Young leaves these possibilities open to interpretation; wisely alluding to such exploration in the 'opening in the hill' or the 'narrow meadow' of his text – the otherwise insurmountable summit of language. Or does he? Maybe we are merely witnessing the atomisation of things *qua* things, as the French poet and dissector of language Francis Ponge[70] would argue; the linguistic exploration and dissection of mere things being permitted to *thing* in their own *thingliness*? A la Ponge's own commonplace *pebbles*, *oysters* and *oranges*, the subject of his many beguiling poems. The microfictions of Joseph Young are all of this and more, existing as a collection of wonderfully crafted oxymora.

The idea of words that wholly exist together as an expression of things, eschewing metaphor, either happy as *things* or openly contradicting this, is echoed further in 'The Gossipers':

The red sweater of her sat with cups empty. Do you want him? said her friend. No, she answered. Just his voice. He, not so far away, spoke. In this way, they invented a machine, her gilt wheels, his explosions. It ran into the night, across several years. Friends regarded it with amusement and teeth. He sat with the red sweater of her. The sun beside you, he said. I know, she answered. Who would invent stories against them?

(*Easter Rabbit*, Publishing Genius Press, 2009, p. 36)

And further still, in 'A Wish':

A pebble sank for 3 days through 3 miles of water. It passed between the skeleton of a whale, in which a school of orange fish lived. When it reached the bottom, it wouldn't move again, missing terribly the sailor's hand.

(*Easter Rabbit*, Publishing Genius Press, 2009, p. 51.)

In 'The Gossipers' all we are left with is 'voice' and just like the subject of her desire, we can't help but want to possess it wholly – it is whilst in our possession that we begin to see how the unique system of image and symbolism is created by Young's deft touch and irregular placement of word: 'red sweater of her', 'cups empty', 'gilt wheels', 'his explosions', 'amusement and teeth', et cetera. Whereas in 'A Wish', Young uses the anthropomorphic tropes of Aesop to give life to his pebble – it becomes more than a mere *thing* (à la Ponge) as it sinks to the bottom of the ocean in a miasma of Aesopic imagery.

Juxtapositions like this abound in *Easter Rabbit*, and it is clear that Joseph Young has had much fun tying these subtle contradictions together for his own amusement. But it also serves another purpose; it displays a sense of language's urgency, its need to convey and our need to understand. We seek meaning in language, even if there is nothing of meaning to convey. We put our trust in language, on one hand a series of sounds and on the other something that underpins the very nature of our being, we walk its fine line in order for it to guide us through life. But what exactly is language, what is it we are so desperate to communicate? What is really happening in 'Lapse', for instance?

Her hand was small enough to thread the fence, touch the bug that held to the wall.

—, she whispered as it fell. *What?* He asked. *What?* She answered. She turned her head, her neck a bracket for the dropping day.

(*Easter Rabbit*, Publishing Genius Press, 2009, p. 66)

Why do we too want to know what it is she whispered? What are we looking for as she dissolves into the same structure of language and symbols we are reading? What did she say? *What?* What in the bug's falling caused her to whisper? Are we too falling through language? Is language falling with us? What is the weight she carries as the world around her drops? *What?*

The attraction of this, and of language as a whole, is that we'll probably never know; which doesn't really matter anyway, because in the above microfiction something quite beautiful has happened, something antediluvian within each of its forty words: a moment has surfaced, a moment in time, which speaks to us of everything and nothing, crystallised in the mythology of its own making. I feel that is what we respond to most when we read 'Lapse', when we too simply *ask*, just like him, just what it is she whispered.

The collection goes on with this exploration. 'Diction' deftly ponders the question and failure of the right word from within the feast of language:

> It was easy to hear the word that turned through the table. It could sound like *death*, or *listen!* or *ridicule*, but it caught at the throat and stuck. The other words, those at the spiked green corners of her eye or the bittersweet planes of his mouth, were pregnant with it, its sons and daughters. They'd labor on, these people, without fruit it seemed, though in fact the table was sweet in the blossoms of it.
>
> (*Easter Rabbit*, Publishing Genius Press, 2009, p. 29)

There is a sense within 'Diction' that we must 'labor on' with the language we have been provided with, carrying the notion that it delivers to us the promise of 'other words' even if these words fail and become stuck in their own formation, we must persist through its 'spiked green corners' and 'bittersweet planes'. Language is 'pregnant', awaiting its own birth with us, we must persevere, and only then will we be able to feast on the 'fruits' of such 'labor', 'sweet in the blossoms of it'. It is the promise of 'other words' that both leads and shapes the development of all communication, whether it be in the form of literature, art, song or any other recognised iteration. It is this same promise that leads us through Young's collection; we need to know what has been said – even if this turns out to be nothing:

> They turned right, off the road, left the smell of the river, the miasma of history. They looked at their hands and fore-arms for dust and scars. *Well?* she said, down the long blue lens of his sight.
>
> ('End', *Easter Rabbit*, Publishing Genius Press, 2009, p. 84)

Joseph Young's microfictions are a necessary step in tracing the influence of the Aesopic tradition throughout literary history, as they contextualise its antiquated tropes in a wholly modern context. There aren't many people in the English-speaking world who write quite like Joseph Young, yet these eighty-six microfic-tions are immediately recognisable to us. In the looping of their mythic and linguistic properties, we can begin to trace the dis-tillation of such unique writing right back to the fables of Aesop – and it is exactly this journey which we, unknowingly, recog-nise. Only then can we begin to trace the process back again, to our own collective sense of time, where the everyday is delivered to us in crystallised fragments of language and text, communi-cated snippets and sound bites of a distant whole, something that was once near to us and has been shattered into myriad pieces and shards of information that can never properly be put back together again. In this context, we can now begin to under-stand the link between Aesop, Robert Walser's *Microscripts*, exceptionally modern writing such as Joseph Young's and the emergence and dissemination of flash fiction via the internet.

Shane Jones:
the novel as contemporary fable

Ever since arguably the first novel, Cervantes' *Don Quixote*, informed its numerous readers that novels don't actually work and instead fail as true representations of reality (something the majority of modern literature's devotees in turn fail to recognise), the more experimentally savvy of novelists throughout the novel's relatively short – and sadly diminishing – history have tried to have fun with this notion, deliberately playing with ideas of the real and unreal within the parameters of language. Novelist Shane Jones is no exception. His hallucinatory short novel, *Light Boxes*, is the epitome of a contemporary fable, displaying many of the recognisable Aesopic tropes I have discussed in this book: otherworldliness, anthropomorphism, exaggerated imagery, fabulist/poetic language, an implied meaning and code, et cetera. Yet it is also an incredibly forward-thinking and modern work of fragmentary, post-fabulist fiction that creates a whole new literary landscape from these tropes, reinventing the contemporary novel's place within modern and popular culture.

In what, then, I would consider to be the first of a new form of fable-as-contemporary-novel[71], *Light Boxes* takes place in a small town in which the month of February has decided that it never wants to end, plunging the town into a seemingly endless winter of more than three hundred days of snow and grey light. All forms of flight, including anything that might take flight, or can be used to take flight, have been banned. This strange law is

155

enforced by a sinister sect of axe-carrying priests who roam the town with nefarious intent, making sure the townsfolk do not dare violate this law. Just when we think things could not get any worse a number of children start to disappear in the middle of the night – most are taken from their own beds – including the main protagonist Thaddeus Lowe's daughter Bianca. Eventually a mysterious group of men begin to appear, dressed in top hats and coloured bird masks, balloonists called 'The Solution' who decide it's time to take action against February and declare war.

The novel is divided up into very short chapters, some only a couple of lines long. It is within these alternate narrations, which read like omniscient nodes hovering around the town, recording everything that's taking place from every conceivable angle by varying characters, that Jones' novel itself begins to take flight. And take flight it does, in bursts of colourful, extraordinarily rich prose that seems weightless in its esoteric conjuring of image and symbolism. Faulknerian[72] in scope, it sweeps through the novel like a kaleidoscopic lens, a projected narrative beaming back the fantastic and the minuscule in equal measure. Early on we begin to see the novel's machinations at work:

Bianca

When I was really little my father came into my bedroom with a sheet of fabric he said would one day fly in the sky.

I'll show you, he said, sitting down on the edge of the bed then sliding towards the middle where I sat with my legs crossed.

Through my bedroom window I watched a tree lose a branch under the weight of snow that had been falling for months. Before the branch hit the ground a sheet of yellow fabric floated down over my eyes. It felt like silk and smelled of oil and stream water.

I heard the clank of metal, and then a hot flamer near the back of my neck, and then the fabric lifted from my face and it bloomed into a giant flower that touched the ceiling and grew towards the corners of my bedroom.

What does this feel like, my father said.

It's like being inside one of those globes the shopkeepers make in town, I said, now standing on the bed, fingertips reaching towards the flower. It feels wonderful, it feels like happiness.

It will be called, my father said, a balloon.

(*Light Boxes*, Hamish Hamilton, 2010, p. 16.)

This is a rather typical chapter to be found in *Light Boxes*, in terms of its fabular tone and fantastic elements. Bianca feels minuscule in a world that makes no sense; there is a desire to take flight from this world, to escape the geometry of her room, to find happiness elsewhere. She is looking back to happier times. She is caught in stasis now and only ever 'feels wonderful' in this world, where the simplest of memories only 'feels like happiness'.

The motif of what is *felt* runs deep throughout the novel. Things are never concrete and feelings seem to hover into view vaguely, it is a strange dream-like world where actions are incredible and feelings have been pushed aside by the magnitude of February's seemingly endless winter. But incredible worlds can create happiness, and the longing for happiness is strong. In many metafictional twists and turns Jones litters the text with numerous clues, codes and ciphers, sometimes inserting lists which serve as signposts, both explicit and quirkily humorous in intention:

List of Artists Who Created Fantasy Worlds to Try and Cure Bouts of Sadness

1. Italo Calvino
2. Garcia Marquez
3. Jim Henson and Borges – Labyrinth(s)
4. The creator of Myspace

5. Richard Brautigan
6. J.K. Rowling
7. The inventor of the Children's toy Lite-Brite
8. D.A. Levy
9. David Foster Wallace
10. Gauguin and the Caribbean
11. Charles Schulz
12. Liam Rector

(*Light Boxes*, Hamish Hamilton, 2010, p. 98)

It's certainly a quirky list (and the entwining of Jim Henson and Jorge Luis Borges is immediately amusing), but it should be taken seriously, too. It perfectly sums up Jones' intentions of creating his own fantasy world, one which conveys the overwhelming urge to become happy and to connect through protection. It's in clues like this that we begin to see that Jones is tapping into something else, the same inner search we find in the numerous Aesopic fables for happiness and companionship, both 'The Eagle and the Farmer' and 'The Shepherd and the Lion' are similar examples of this.

Jones sets up his protagonist Thaddeus as the classic reluctant hero called into adventure, an archetype that is found in many of the monomyths[73] throughout the history of western narrative (also think a process of *individuation*,[74] for a psychological example):

Thaddeus

The Solution came to my window last night. They had on their bird masks and black top hats. They wore a single brown scarf around their necks. I said I understood the need to rebel and protect our town against February. I reminded them of the tactics used last year.

Most importantly, they said, think of your daughter, Bianca. I saw that some snow had gathered in a corner on the ceiling. I grabbed a broom to sweep it away.

When I turned back around, The Solution was walking away into the snowfall. It looked like they were skipping. I closed my eyes. I imagined Selah and Bianca in a canoe so narrow they had to lie down with their arms folded on their stomachs, their heads at opposite ends, their toes touching. I dreamed two miniature suns. I set one each upon their foreheads. I dreamed a waterfall and a calm lake of my arms below to catch them.

(*Light Boxes*, Hamish Hamilton, 2010, p. 21)

Thaddeus knows what needs to be done, but he is fearful, overly protective and at first reluctant. Instead of thinking about how he can help The Solution in their planned rebellion, instead his thoughts turn immediately to his wife and daughter. He dreams of them being taken away to safety in a canoe, a warm sun protecting them both. We see the cold winter disappear as Thaddeus trains his thoughts upon them, creating an image of neo-biblical/Egyptian significance, where the symbolism of both the sun and water were/are used for protection against evil, signifying cleansing and purity. Furthermore, the Egyptian sun god Ra (or Ré), represented by light, warmth and growth, was thought to have travelled on boats which connected him to both the sky and the underworld.

Offset from this symbolic language and just as steeped in its mythologies and the otherworldliness of its milieu is the ever-increasing anthropomorphisation of the month of February. Throughout *Light Boxes* February is more than just a month, it becomes a living and breathing thing with feelings and emotion, evoking its own form of sadness. Jones peppers *Light Boxes* with discarded lists that February has written himself in moments of contemplation and despair, infusing the narrative with a faux sense of real feeling – it is only when we remember that this is a list supposedly written by the month of February that the rug is pulled from underneath us:

Short List Found in February's Back Pocket

1. I've done everything I can.
2. I need to know you won't leave.
3. I wrote a story to show love and it turned to war.
How awful.
4. I twisted myself around stars and poked the moon
where the moon couldn't reach.
5. I'm the kind of person who kidnaps children and takes
flight away.

(*Light Boxes*, Hamish Hamilton, 2010, p. 67)

Soon enough February is revealed to us in his corporeal, human form. He is portrayed as a physically pathetic human being whose very sadness has caused the prolonged winter in the town. He is visualised to us through the eyes of 'the girl who smelled of smoke and honey':

FEBRUARY SAT ON A COTTAGE FLOOR
with the girl who smelled of smoke and honey. The girl was telling him that she was tired of being around someone who carried so much sadness in his body. February drew his kneecaps to his eye sockets.

February apologized, he rocked back and forth. When he stretched his legs back out the girl was smiling and running in place. February asked what she was doing. The girl who smelled of honey and smoke said it was to cheer him up.

I don't think that's going to work, said February. I'm sorry but it just won't.
Just try it, said the girl who smelled of honey and smoke. Please.

February stood up and ran in place. His joints popped. He bumped into a table, knocking over a jug of water.
Looks like a flood, said the girl who smelled of honey and smoke, who pumped her legs and arms faster.

It does, said February, who watched the water expand across the table and drip onto the floor with great delight.

(*Light Boxes*, Hamish Hamilton, 2010, p. 62)

Through her eyes February cuts a pathetic, sad figure, sitting hunched, his knees drawn and tucked in close to his chest, his head bowed contemplating his own sadness, his wrong-doings and the negative impact they have had on the townsfolk. February sits, lost in his sadness; he 'rocks back and forth' like a man with a troubled mind – things sit uneasily within him. The anthropomorphisation of February firmly places *Light Boxes* in the realms of the literary fable – it is both the oldest and clever-est of tricks for Jones to use. Thick with Jones' quirky humour; it allows us to observe without feeling any distance, without upsetting us. We allow the improbability of the whole chapter to speak to us, we understand these human qualities, and through them we begin to understand the psychological implications of the entire novel.

So, can a contemporary fable such as *Light Boxes* be classified as a contemporary novel? Some critics have argued its power as an elongated metaphor for creativity blocked by a world we find unfamiliar and confusing, others have noted it being a story about family, and the strange bonds we are forced to make to help keep them safe. I would rather like it to exist on its own terms, a novel as fable, and vice versa, that is able to shed light on whatever it is we look at, because it speaks to us in the same way that all good fables do, no matter how far-fetched or magical and hallucinatory they at first may seem: in a language we can truly understand.

Tania Hershman:
from Aesop to flash fiction

It seems to me that in flash fiction we have come full circle and, once again, in one of our most modern forms of literature, the oldest of influences looms large – enlivening it in a modern context. The emergence of flash fiction in modern culture owes as much to the internet as it does to the thread of Aesop's influence throughout modern literature – this thread is indeed tangible in the wealth of fabulous flash fiction stories published each day online around the world. One only has to visit sites such as *flashfiction.net* and *smokelong.com*[75] or journals such as *Matter: The Journal of Compressed Creative Arts*[76] to get a real sense of some of the most electrifying and ground-breaking flash fiction published today; displaying work from authors all around the world who manage to compress the weird, the fabulous and the truly astonishing into their fictions. It seems to me that fabulist literature has found its home both online and in the compressed micro-world of flash fiction writing. The term 'flash fiction'[77] is used to describe a multitude of genres and modes of writing, as well as the more formal and traditional modes of short story writing, such as prose poetry, fables, myths, ghost stories, parables, fairy tales, horror and science fiction. The term also spans numerous theoretical and highly experimental techniques such as postmodernism, surrealism, fabulism, postfabulism, realism and magic realism. Such writing seems to exist in the space between the parameters of the more established and well-worn forms of expression set by poetry and prose; slipping in and out of view, often seeming both askew and remarkable in its brevity and conciseness of expression.

It is widely acknowledged that this oldest of forms has seen its re-emergence in the rise of the internet, and the publishing of literature, short stories and fiction in its never-ending array of online literary journals. It seems the brevity of flash fiction is a perfect match for the average internet reader, it can happily sit on the screen without the reader having to scroll down every few minutes. Most exciting of all is flash fiction's ability to become mobile content, as publishing increasingly becomes XML dominated – we can read flash fiction on our iPhones, iPads and Kindles in transit, for example. This doesn't mean to say it is a solely digitised genre, it's not; there are plenty of print anthologies around, and individual authors' collections to choose from, too. It's just that in an ever-more digitised world of mobile snippets of content to be devoured where and when we choose in the palms of our hands, flash fiction seems to have found its small place amongst the rising tide of technological innovations.

In recent history flash fiction has had many surprising exponents, who we could say have produced fictions that can be labelled as flash fiction in today's terms, providing us with an example of the genre's depth and influence; they include novelists, poets and writers such as Richard Brautigan, Guy de Maupassant, Anton Chekhov, O. Henry, Italo Calvino, Raymond Carver, Ernest Hemingway, Franz Kafka, John Updike and Joyce Carol Oates, to name more than a few. Modern flash fiction writers include up and coming authors such as Grace Paley, Barry Yourgrau, Stefanie Freele, Peter Orner, Etgar Keret, Lydia Davies, Vanessa Gibble, Sarah Hilary, David Gaffney and Sara Crowley. As you can see it's a vibrant scene – and this is only the tip of the iceberg. Obviously, there are far too many writers of flash fiction around for me to concentrate on in this chapter so I will discuss the work of just one whom I feel is developing and expanding the genre in new and exciting ways, whilst also displaying some of its Aesopic roots in the process.

Best known for her award-winning collection *The White Road and Other Stories*,[78] Tania Hershman is also a prolific flash fiction writer (and tutor). A science journalist for some time, before turning to full-time fiction writing, Hershman's longer fictions are concerned with the marrying of the stark science of physics with the more human emotional realms, such as the individual experience of both loss and desire.

Hershman's flash fiction output is staggering and it is clear that it is a genre that she clearly loves, such is the breadth of styles and contexts she is willing to explore. In 'Inchworms', for example, we see a mixing of fabulist imagery with a deep-felt human dichotomy:

> Another day brings inchworms in to see me, in their droves, they inch so slowly, slowly forwards. I want a word, I tell them, just one word, my pilgrim self notes down it all, a code for stitching sounds together. But the inchworms bring cracked shells, twigs and things of no damn use to me.
>
> I think in quotes as if you listened to my thoughts. You don't, you are not there, so even if I 'dreamt about you,' just like that, you would not hear me. Even if I 'loved you from afar,' you would not know. Even if I walked about me, room to room and 'swore undying' to you, you would not reply. At night, the moon and stars turn up to laugh at me, skimming overhead from tree to twig, and I, 'my heart so softly breaking,' ask for help, but they just head for home, and leave me, inching slowly, slowly forwards.

(*Inchworms*, *The Pedestal Magazine*, Issue 53,
www.thepedastalmagazine.com)

First, we are struck by the imagery of the inchworm, quite literally the caterpillar of Geometer moths (or *Geometridae*),[79] giving us a sense of a forthcoming metamorphosis, but this imagery also taps into something deeper, and far more mythic and lyrical, a loop to something deep-rooted, some distant desire. Just like in the rudimentary arithmetic of the song 'The Inch Worm', written by Frank Loesser[80] and featured in the biopic of Hans Christian Andersen (a notable fabulist), the subject of *Inchworms* feeds the desire to build something from the accumulation of something else – in this case the words she needs to formulate the right sentence or 'a code for stitching sound together'. But thought is processed in snippets, in 'quotes', and nothing seems complete, the other is not there to 'listen' and only the inchworms' progress counts, until the eventual metamorphosis. The loop occurs at the end; an imagined metamorphosis, where she becomes the inchworm 'inching slowly, slowly forwards', towards the same metamorphosis repeated; only this time, it's a metamorphosis from the arithmetic of waiting into a pure geometry of freedom and love.

In the moving 'A Sigh Rose Inside Him', a whole new set of emotions are dealt with, ones of regret, loss and longing:

It was her, standing there outside the café in the rain, bareheaded. He knew, from the way she stood, her hands shattered by raindrops, her fingers turned up to catch, her face fetchingly flushed in the damp. He was not a good man, or noble, or important. But she was there for him, of that he was certain. And so he approached.

As he stood near enough, but not too much, she turned away from him as if someone had called her name. He took in the back of her head, the slicked down hair, like a dog, he thought then, and held himself back from following the thought. He didn't want to compare her to any other living thing, or dead. He reached out to almost her shoulder.

'I'm sorry,' he said and when she didn't move, he stepped another step towards and, his throat itching, said it again.

Her face, when it was in front of him, was the face of some-one he had known but never met and a sigh rose inside him.

'I'm sorry,' he said a third time, 'for the weather, and isn't it a shame?' and his own hands made motions as if to express more. When she smiled, the steely clouds that had been clos-ing in on his heart, shifted and cleared. And when she spoke, they dissolved into powder which sifted and sparkled through his toes.

('A Sigh Rose Inside Him', *Pank Magazine*, February 2009, www.pankmagazine.com)

There is a fabulist element at play in this otherwise rather tradi-tional story, where characters' words dissolve 'into powder' and hands are 'shattered' by the raindrops and people cannot be com-pared to 'anything living, or dead'. Interwoven with these fant-astic elements is a heartfelt breakdown of communication, where the words 'I'm sorry' are never enough to convey the intended sense of regret and atonement – where what is meant to be said is replaced by vagaries and clichés such as the weather in order to hide the failure to express emotion. Without words we are merely strangers; we are a series of sighs caught deep, unable to blossom into the petals of a rose.

'I Am a Camera' exhibits by far a more modern approach in technique and structure, displaying the machinations and pro-cessing of an almost machine-like mind on the verge of malfunc-tion:

'I am a camera,' she whispered to herself in the shower, slid-ing her fingers along the rail already installed for the day when she wouldn't be able to find her way out. She thought of herself as one of those devices with a photographer hid-ing under a cloth, producing sepia-washed pictures. She clicked and whirred and stored images inside, cataloguing scenes from her memory. Faces and landscapes, each titled for easy access, later on.

When the day came, the shutters of her camera floundered against the darkness. She sat still, noises pressing around her, and opened her photo album. 'May 1st, Brighton, me and Simon,' she murmured, and her inside eye saw the colours and textures. Images came up and she bid them. 'Stay with me,' she whispered, the pixels dancing on the inside of her eyelids. She gripped the arms of the chair. 'Stay with me,' she demanded, but the colours were already starting to fade.

('I Am a Camera', *The White Road and Other Stories*, Salt Publishing, 2008, p. 25)

Memory in this piece of fiction is seen as a series of photographic images that have been taken and catalogued by the mind's eye. Just as in the pre-digitised techniques used to develop photography; or an electronic file prone to corrupt over time, or self-destruct entirely, our memories are prone to decay. Structurally, Hershman divides the piece into two sections: a positive image and a negative. This juxtaposition gives the fiction both weight and direction: every positive image also has its negative. Upon reading the title of this piece I was immediately put in mind of Jean-Philippe Toussaint's wonderful novel *Camera*, which employs a similar use of metaphor: as a mechanism to help frame our struggle in coping with the reality around us. Like the camera in Toussaint's novel, which his protagonist throws into the murky sea at night, 'having temporarily given up fighting a seemingly inexhaustible reality'[81] and hoping the pictures will fade into the blackness of the sea, Hershman's camera is one of increasing despair, struggling with its inability to defeat reality around it, although this time not by throwing it away, but by trying to capture it for ever – keeping it out of the shadows.

In a fine example of just what can be achieved using an economy of words, 'Heart' displays in its simple, fabular tone, a weightiness and deep-rooted power of representation that some longer fictions either struggle to achieve at all, or completely over-egg in their desire to convey such imagery:

> She drew her hands out of the chest cavity and looked at the clock.
>
> 'Time of death,' she said.
>
> In her locker room, she stripped off her bloodied scrubs and put on clothes for the real world. Then she left the hospital and turned the corner, rain flattening her hair.
>
> At Sammy's, she sat at the bar, lit a cigarette and ordered a drink. When it came, she exhaled through her mouth, touched her fingertips to the rim of the glass, and remembered how it was to have a man's heart beat itself out in the cup of her palms.
>
> ('Heart', *The White Road and Other Stories*, Salt Publishing, 2008, p. 85)

Isn't this the simple sum and totality of all human existence right here, held in the palms of her hands? Tania Hershman's shorter fictions – and the genre of flash fiction in general – display all the hallmarks of Aesop's blueprint, the same blueprint that can be traced throughout each and every work mentioned in this book. It is an ontological blueprint that maps out all of our loves and fears, hopes and dreams; a foundation that has helped to galvanise the assimilation of narrative into the mind-bogglingly complex culture of our simple everyday, ordinary lives. It is staggering just how far the influence of Aesop has penetrated into our narratives and mythologies, strengthening the building blocks of our fictions – the sum and total of our continued struggle with the communication of our, at once confusing and exhilarating, collective existence.

Just as the fables of Aesop help us not only to reimagine the ordinary lives and contemporary culture of ancient Greece, but to immerse ourselves in its philosophies, laws, customs and myriad idiosyncrasies, flash fiction and fabulist literature in general allows us a glimpse into the workings of our own daily lives;

from how we feel, live and communicate with one another through the languages we have been passed down, to our re-imagining of the world around us through this very same language. Fables have given us the blueprint to document the everyday in fantastic ways, in ways which immediately appeal or confuse and terrorise us. They give structure to our thoughts and facilitate the communication of our daydreams, our nightmares, the creations of our vast imaginations – from the multitudinous intricacies of Joyce's *Finnegans Wake* to the hard-hitting simplicity of Hemingway's 'Baby Shoes',[82] the same influence born out of Aesop's gift of speech looms large.

Fables have served us for two thousand years or more and continue to say everything there is to say about us as we carry on drinking from the deep well of their creation. I wish I had all the time in the world to keep on tracing the influence of this most beguiling of narratives, I wish I could have written about many more of the fabulous writers touched by Aesop's brilliance, but time being time I don't. And, if I'm honest, that doesn't matter, because we are each creating our own fables every day, in the lives we live; and somewhere here, near or far, no matter how obscure they may at first seem, someone is writing them down for us. We simply need to look in the right places and all will be fabulously revealed.

Notes

1. Top Ten novels, The Book Depository, 18 September 2007.
2. The sculptor Lysippus was born and worked in Sicyon and famously became the portrait-maker of Alexander the Great.
3. Herman Melville, *Bartleby the Scrivener*, Hesperus Press, 2007, p. 11.
4. Samuel Beckett, *Worstward Ho*, John Calder, 1983, p. 7.
5. For a more detailed exploration of the literature of the 'NO' please see: Enrique Vila-Matas, *Bartleby & Co.*, The Harvill Press, 2004.
6. The Roman version has looser rules than its Greek predecessor iambic trimeter.
7. Often referred to as 'lame iambic' as the stresses are reversed towards the last few beats at the end of a line or stanza, which can sometimes wrong-foot the reader.
8. Hilding Kjellman, *La Vie Seint Edmund le Rei: poème anglo-normand du XIIe siècle par Denis Piramus*. Göteborg: Elanders Boktryckeri Aktiebolag, 1935.
9. *Marie de France: Fables*, ed. and trans. Harriet Spiegel, University of Toronto Press, 1995.
10. *Marie de France: Fables*, ed. and trans. Harriet Spiegel, University of Toronto Press, 1995.
11. The Company of Merchant Adventurers of London, founded in 1407 and London's leading guild of overseas merchants.
12. A series of literary meetings were held between the four which are now embedded in the annals of French literary history and folklore.
13. *Fables: Jean de La Fontaine*, trans. Gordon Pirie, Hesperus Press, 2008.
14. *Fables: Jean de La Fontaine*, trans. Gordon Pirie, Hesperus Press, 2008.
15. *Fables: Jean de La Fontaine*, trans. Gordon Pirie, Hesperus Press, 2008.
16. *Fables: Jean de La Fontaine*, trans. Gordon Pirie, Hesperus Press, 2008.
17. Gabriel Josipovici, *What Ever Happened to Modernism?*, Yale University Press, 2010, p. 158.
18. Virginia Woolf, *The Common Reader*, Mariner Books, 1984.
19. See Benjamin Kunkel, 'Still Small Voice: the fiction of Robert Walser', *The New Yorker*, August 6th, 2007.
20. See Walter Benjamin, 'Robert Walser', trans. Rodney Livingstone. *Das Tagebuch*, 1929.
21. Robert Walser died whilst out on one of his daily walks. His body (together with the eerie imprint of his final footsteps) was found face down in the snow. There are numerous photographs on the internet which have prompted many artists to feature this image in their work, most notably in a series of paintings by the British artist Billy Childish.
22. Robert Walser, 'Introduction', *Microscripts*, New Directions / Christine Burgin, 2010, pp. 9–23.

23. Stewart Home's early novels such as *Slow Death* and *Blow Job* juxtaposed the pulp/*youthspolitation* fictions of Richard Allen with the didactics of Marx, or the deconstruction of Derrida, for example.

24. W.G. Sebald, 'Introduction: "Le Promeneur Solitaire",' trans. Jo Catling in Robert Walser, *The Tanners*, trans. Susan Bernofsky. New Directions, 2009, p. 12.

25. We only have to read the poetry of Paul Celan to grasp a sense of this traumatic experience.

26. David Foster Wallace, 'Some Remarks On Kafka's Funniness From Which Probably Not Enough Has Been Removed', *Consider The Lobster*, Abacus, 2005, p. 64–5.

27. From Latin *fabulosus* 'celebrated in fable; rich in myths' from Latin *fabula* 'fable'.

28. Kafka's own *struggle* is documented with equal measures of pain and beauty in his diaries.

29. Knut Hamsun's novel is considered to be the first work of early Modernism.

30. James Joyce, *Finnegans Wake*, Penguin Books, 1992 edn, p. 378.29.

31. James Joyce, *Finnegans Wake*, Penguin Books, 1992 edn, pp. 148–68.

32. 'An Analysis of the Mind of James Joyce', *The Enemy*, January 1927.

33. James Joyce, *Finnegans Wake*, Penguin Books, 1992 edn, p. 416.3.

34. James Joyce, *Dubliners*, 1914.

35. James Joyce, *Finnegans Wake*, Penguin Books, 1992 edn, p. 417.3.

36. Fable 125, *Aesop's Fables*, trans. Laura Gibbs, Oxford World's Classics, 2002.

37. Joyce, James, *Finnegans Wake*, Penguin Books, 1992 edn, p. 1.

38. Arthur Schopenhauer, *The World as Will and Idea*, Everyman Paperback, 1995.

39. Maya is an Indian deity that appears in Hindu, Buddhist and Sikh mythology serving to govern an illusion and dream of duality within the universe.

40. Samuel Beckett, 'Dante… Bruno… Vico… Joyce', *Disjecta*, Calder Publications, 1983, p. 27.

41. Giambattista Vico was an Italian political philosopher and historian. In *The New Science* (1725) Vico developed the *ricorso* (recurring cycle) of the three ages: the divine, the heroic, and the human.

42. James Joyce, *Finnegans Wake*, Penguin Books, 1992 edn, p. 414.31.

43. Henri Bergson was one of the most influential French philosophers of the nineteenth century. His essays dealing with our collective theory of time all appear in *The Creative Mind: An Introduction to Metaphysics*, Kensington Publishing Corp., 1946.

44. James Joyce, *Finnegans Wake*, Penguin Books, 1992 edn, p. 471.6.

45. James Joyce, *Finnegans Wake*, Penguin Books, 1992 edn, p. 471.21–2.

46. James Joyce, *Finnegans Wake*, Penguin Books, 1992 edn, P. 416.5.

47. James Joyce, *Finnegans Wake*, Penguin Books, 1992 edn, p. 378.29.

48. Jorge Luis Borges, 'Epilogue', *Other Inquisitions*, trans. Ruth L.C Simms, University of Texas Press, 1975.

49. James E. Irby, 'Introduction', *Labyrinths*, Penguin Classics, 2000.

50. James E. Irby, 'Introduction', *Labyrinths*, Penguin Classics, 2000.

51. 'Borges and I', *Labyrinths*, trans. James E. Irby, Penguin Classics, 2000, p. 282–3,

52. Thomas Bernhard, *The Voice Imitator*, University of Chicago Press, 1998 (*Der Stimmenimitator*, Suhrkamp Verlag Frankfurt am Main, 1978).

53. Bernhard, Thomas, *The Voice Imitator*, University of Chicago Press, 1998 (*Der Stimmenimitator*, Suhrkamp Verlag Frankfurt am Main, 1978).

54. Maurice Blanchot, 'Everyday Speech', Yale French Studies, No 73, *Everyday Life*, 1987, trans. Susan Hanson, pp. 12–20.

55. 'Everyday Speech', Yale French Studies, No 73, *Everyday Life*, 1987, trans. Susan Hanson, pp. 12–20.

56. Gilles Deleuze and Félix Guattari, 'The Whole and its Parts', *Anti-Oedipus*, trans. Robert Hurley, Mark Seem, and Helen R. Lane, The Athlone Press, 1984, p. 42.

57. Henri Lefebvre, a chronicler of the everyday, his notable work being *La vie quotidienne dans le monde*, Gallimard, 1962; *Everyday Life in the Modern World*, trans. Sacha Rabinovitch, Harper and Row, 1971.

58. Maurice Blanchot, 'Everyday Speech', Yale French Studies, No 73, trans. Susan Hanson, *Everyday Life*, 1987, p. 12–20.

59. Maurice Blanchot, 'Everyday Speech', Yale French Studies, No 73, trans. Susan Hanson, *Everyday Life*, 1987, p. 12–20.

60. See the first joint INS 'Declaration on Inauthenticity', Tom McCarthy, Simon Critchley, Drawing Center, New York, 2009.

61. Jorge Luis Borges, 'Kafka and his Precursors', *Labyrinths*, trans. James E. Irby, Penguin Classics, 2000, pp. 234–7.

62. See short text 'La Falaise', *Celui qui ne peut se servir de mots*, Montpellier, Fata Morgana, 1975, and the essay 'Les Peintres de l'empêchement', *Disjecta, Miscellaneous Writings and a Dramatic Fragment*, Calder Publications, London, 1983, pp. 133–8.

63. Again see 'La Falaise'.

64. HP Tinker, *The Swank Bisexual Wine Bar of Modernity*, Social Disease Books, 2007.

65. UK-based literary and artwork quarterly, edited by London paediatrician and author Dr Martin Bax since 1959 (www.amabitmagazine.co.uk).

66. François Rabelais (c. 1494–1553) was a Renaissance Humanist writer of fantasy, satire, the grotesque and bawdy ballads. His most popular work is *Gargantua and Pantagruel*.

67. Benjamin Tabart was responsible for first publishing the popular fairy tale *Jack and the Beanstalk* in 1807. Although published anonymously, his

version was most probably based on popular oral retellings of the time.

68. Douglas Holt and Douglas Cameron, *Cultural Strategy: Using Innovative Ideologies to Build Breakthrough Brands*, OUP, 2010, p.252.

69. See interview with Joseph Young at *The Short Review* (www.theshortreview.com).

70. Ponge's two most important collections are *Le Parti pris des choses* and *Pièces*. I would also recommend the recent collection *Unfinished Odes to Mud*, (trans. Beverley Brahic, CB Editions, 2009) which combines decent English translations from both these seminal collections.

71. A form of novel that embraces the fabulous over the literary, whilst still maintaining its own literary standing.

72. Many critics have compared Jones' narrative technique in *Light Boxes* to the myriad and alternate points of view in William Faulkner's seminal novel *As I Lay Dying*. A comparison with which I would concur wholeheartedly.

73. See Joseph Campbell's seminal work *The Hero with a Thousand Faces*. Incidentally, Campbell borrowed the term *monomyth* from Joyce's *Finnegans Wake*.

74. *Individuation* is the name given to the process of a development of the self, from a fragmented undifferentiated state, towards completing its individual personality as a whole. See Carl Jung's *Man and his Symbols* and Northrop Frye's *Anatomy of Criticism*.

75. In China, flash fiction is commonly known as 'Smoke-Long' as it takes about the length of time to smoke a cigarette as it does to read a story.

76. See www.matterpress.com

77. The term is thought to have been coined by the publication of the following anthology: *Flash Fiction: Seventy-two Very Short Stories*, eds. James Thomas, Denise Thomas and Tom Hazuka, 1992.

78. Tania Hershman, *The White Road and Other Stories*, Salt Publishing, 2008.

79. The caterpillars are sometimes called *loopers*, or *spanworms*, along with *inchworms* due to the loop that is formed as they move.

80. The song was originally performed by Danny Kaye, but has since become a staple song in children's TV programmes such as *The Muppets* and *Sesame Street* performed by many artists; a classic fable-like song about measurement and arithmetic:

Two and two are four / Four and four are eight / Eight and eight are sixteen / Sixteen and sixteen are thirty-two / Inch worm, inch worm / measuring the marigolds / You and your arithmetic / You'll probably go far / Inch worm, inch worm / measuring the marigolds / Seems to me you'll stop and see / How beautiful they are.

81. Jean-Philippe Toussaint, *Camera*, trans. Matthew B. Smith, Dalkey Archive Press, 2008.

82. One of the shortest and most powerful works of fiction ever written, by Ernest Hemingway: *'For sale: baby shoes. Never worn.'*

Bibliography

1. Barks, Coleman. *Rumi: Bridge to the Soul*. London: HarperCollins; 2007.
2. Barlow, Francis. *Life of Aesop*. London; 1687.
3. Beckett, Samuel. 'La Falaise' *Celui qui ne peut se servir de mots*. France: Montpellier, Fata Morgana; 1975.
4. Beckett, Samuel. *Disjecta*. London: Calder Publications; 1983.
5. Beckett, Samuel. *Worstward Ho*. London: Calder Publications; 1983.
6. Benjamin, Walter. 'Robert Walser' [Rodney Livingstone, trans]. Das Tagebuch. Germany; 1929.
7. Bergson, Henri. *The Creative Mind: An Introduction to Metaphysics*. New York: Kensington Publishing Corp; 1946.
8. Bernhard, Thomas. *The Voice Imitator* [Kenneth J. Northcott, trans]. USA: University of Chicago Press; 1997.
9. Blanchot, Maurice. 'Everyday Speech' [Susan Hanson, trans]. Yale French Studies. 1987; (73):12–20.
10. Borges, Jorge Luis. *Labyrinths* [James E. Irby, trans]. London: Penguin Classics; 2000.
11. Borges, Jorge Luis. *Other Inquisitions* [Ruth L.C. Simms, trans]. USA: University of Texas Press; 1975.
12. Butler, Blake. *Ever*. USA: Calamari Press; 2009.
13. Campbell, Joseph. *A Skeleton Key to 'Finnegans Wake'*. USA: New World Library; 2005.
14. Campbell, Joseph. *The Hero With A Thousand Faces*. USA: Fontana Press; 1993.
15. Caxton, William [Jacobs, Joseph, ed.]. *The Fables of Aesop, as first printed by William Caxton in 1484, with those of Avian, Alfonso and Po*. USA: BiblioBazaar; 2009.
16. Deleuze, Gilles, Guattari, Félix. *Anti-Oedipus* [Hurley, R., Seem, M., Lane, H.R., trans]. London: The Athlone Press; 1984.
17. de La Fontaine, Jean. *Fables: Jean de La Fontaine* [Gordon Pirie, trans]. London: Hesperus Press; 2008.
18. Frye, Northrop. *Anatomy of Criticism: Four Essays*. USA: Princeton University Press; 1992.
19. Hershman, Tania. *The White Road and Other Stories*. UK: Salt Publishing; 2008.
20. Holt, Douglas, Cameron, Douglas. *Cultural Strategy: Using Innovative Ideologies to Build Breakthrough Brands*, Oxford, UK: Oxford University Press; 2010.
21. Jacobs, John C. [trans]. *The fables of Odo of Cheriton*. USA: Syracuse University Press; 1985.

22. Jacobs, Joseph [trans.], *Aesop's Fables, Selected, told anew and their history traced by Joseph Jacobs*, London: Macmillan & Co, 1894.

23. Jolas, Eugene (ed.) *Transition*. 1929; (16/17).

24. Jones, Shane. *Light Boxes*. London: Hamish Hamilton; 2010.

25. Josipovici, Gabriel. *What Ever Happened to Modernism?* USA: Yale University Press; 2010.

26. Joyce, James. *Finnegans Wake*. London: Penguin Books; 1992.

27. Joyce, James. *Dubliners*. London: Minerva Paperbacks; 1992.

28. Jung, Carl. *Man and his Symbols*. London: Picador; 1978.

29. Kafka, Franz. *The Great Wall of China and other short works* [Malcolm Pasley, trans]. London: Penguin Modern Classics; 2002.

30. Kjellman, Hilding. *La Vie Seint Edmund le Rei: poème anglo-normand du XIIe siècle par Denis Piramus*. Göteborg: Elanders Boktryckeri Aktiebolag; 1935.

31. Lefebvre, Henri. *Everyday Life in the Modern World* [Sacha Rabinovitch, trans]. London: Harper and Row; 1971.

32. Lewis, Wyndham. *Time and Western Man*. USA: Black Sparrow Press; 1993.

33. Martin, Mary Lou [trans]. *The Fables of Marie de France: An English Translation*. USA: Summa Publications; 1984.

34. Melville, Herman. *Bartleby the Scrivener*. London: Hesperus Press; 2007.

35. Nietzsche, Friedrich. *Thus Spoke Zarathustra* [R.J. Hollingdale, trans]. London: Penguin Classics; 1969.

36. Pascal, Blaise. *Pensées* [A. Krailsheimer, trans]. London: Penguin Classics; 2003.

37. Perry, Ben Edwin [ed.]. *Aesopica: A Series of Texts Relating to Aesop of Ascribed to Him*. 2nd edition. USA: University of Illinois Press; 2007.

38. Plato. *Phaedo* [F. J. Church, trans]. USA: The Library of Liberal Arts. The Bobbs-Merrill Company inc; 1951.

39. Plato. *Phaedrus* [W.C. Helmbold, trans]. USA: The Library of Liberal Arts. The Bobbs-Merrill Company, inc; 1951.

40. Plutarch. *Moralia*. Vol. II. USA: Loeb Classical Library. Harvard University Press; 1928.

41. Ponge, Francis. *Unfinished Odes to Mud* [Beverley Brahic, trans]. London: CB Editions; 2009.

42. Schimmel, Annemarie. *Rumi's World: The Life and Work of the Great Sufi Poet*. USA: Shambhala Publications Inc; 2002.

43. Schopenhauer, Arthur. *The World as Will and Idea*. USA: Everyman Paperback; 1995.

44. Sebald, W. G. 'Introduction: Le Promeneur Solitaire'. In Walser, Robert. *The Tanners* [Susan Bernofsky, trans]. USA: New Directions; 2009. p. 12.

45. Smart, Christopher [trans.], *A Poetical Translation of the Fables of Phaedrus*. London; 1765.

46. Spiegel, Harriet [trans]. *Marie de France: Fables*. Canada: University

of Toronto Press; 1995.

47. Stevenson, William. *Life of William Caxton: With an Account of the Invention of Printing*. USA: Kessinger Publishing; 2009.

48. Tinker, HP. *The Dead Palace*. *Ambit*. Autumn 2005 (182):19–28.

49. Tinker, HP. *The Swank Bisexual Wine Bar of Modernity*. London: Social Disease Books; 2007.

50. Thomas, Denise, Thomas, James, Hazuka, Tom [eds]. *Flash Fiction: Seventy-Two Very Short Stories*. USA: W. W. Norton & Company; 1992.

51. Toussaint, Jean-Philippe. *Camera* [Matthew B. Smith, trans]. USA: Dalkey Archive Press; 2008.

52. Wallace, David Foster. 'Some Remarks On Kafka's Funniness From Which Probably Not Enough Has Been Removed'. USA: Abacus; 2005. Chapter 3, Consider The Lobster and Other Essays; pp. 60–6.

53. Walser, Robert. *Jakob von Gunten* [Christopher Middleton, trans]. USA: New York Review Books Classics; 1999.

54. Walser, Robert. *Microscripts* [Susan Bernofsky, trans]. USA: New Directions/Christine Burgin; 2010.

55. Walser, Robert. *The Robbers* [Susan Bernofsky, trans]. USA: University of Nebraska Press; 2000.

56. Woolf, Virginia. *The Common Reader*. USA: Mariner Books. Houghton Mifflin Harcourt; 1984.

57. Young, Joseph. *Easter Rabbit*. USA: Publishing Genius Press; 2009.

Acknowledgements

I would like to thank Dr Brian Sudlow of the University of Reading for the initial nudges in the right direction; Ellie Robins for her ideas; Martha Pooley at Hesperus Press for her diligent editing; Stephen Mitchelmore for the advice; Niven Govinden, Nikesh Shukla, Gavin James Bower and Stuart Evers for their support; and finally Holly Ahern, my unwavering inspiration.

HESPERUS PRESS

Hesperus Press is committed to bringing near what is far – far both in space and time. Works written by the greatest authors, and unjustly neglected or simply little known in the English-speaking world, are made accessible through new translations and a completely fresh editorial approach. Through these classic works, the reader is introduced to the greatest writers from all times and all cultures.

For more information on Hesperus Press, please visit our website: **www.hesperuspress.com**

SELECTED TITLES FROM HESPERUS PRESS

Author	Title	Foreword writer
Pietro Aretino	*The School of Whoredom*	Paul Bailey
Pietro Aretino	*The Secret Life of Nuns*	
Jane Austen	*Lesley Castle*	Zoë Heller
Jane Austen	*Love and Friendship*	Fay Weldon
Honoré de Balzac	*Colonel Chabert*	A.N. Wilson
Charles Baudelaire	*On Wine and Hashish*	Margaret Drabble
Giovanni Boccaccio	*Life of Dante*	A.N. Wilson
Charlotte Brontë	*The Spell*	
Emily Brontë	*Poems of Solitude*	Helen Dunmore
Mikhail Bulgakov	*Fatal Eggs*	Doris Lessing
Mikhail Bulgakov	*The Heart of a Dog*	A.S. Byatt
Giacomo Casanova	*The Duel*	Tim Parks
Miguel de Cervantes	*The Dialogue of the Dogs*	Ben Okri
Geoffrey Chaucer	*The Parliament of Birds*	
Anton Chekhov	*The Story of a Nobody*	Louis de Bernières
Anton Chekhov	*Three Years*	William Fiennes
Wilkie Collins	*The Frozen Deep*	
Joseph Conrad	*Heart of Darkness*	A.N. Wilson
Joseph Conrad	*The Return*	Colm Tóibín
Gabriele D'Annunzio	*The Book of the Virgins*	Tim Parks
Dante Alighieri	*The Divine Comedy: Inferno*	
Dante Alighieri	*New Life*	Louis de Bernières
Daniel Defoe	*The King of Pirates*	Peter Ackroyd
Marquis de Sade	*Incest*	Janet Street-Porter
Charles Dickens	*The Haunted House*	Peter Ackroyd
Charles Dickens	*A House to Let*	
Fyodor Dostoevsky	*The Double*	Jeremy Dyson
Fyodor Dostoevsky	*Poor People*	Charlotte Hobson
Alexandre Dumas	*One Thousand and One Ghosts*	

George Eliot	*Amos Barton*	Matthew Sweet
Henry Fielding	*Jonathan Wild the Great*	Peter Ackroyd
F. Scott Fitzgerald	*The Popular Girl*	Helen Dunmore
Gustave Flaubert	*Memoirs of a Madman*	Germaine Greer
Ugo Foscolo	*Last Letters of Jacopo Ortis*	Valerio Massimo Manfredi
Elizabeth Gaskell	*Lois the Witch*	Jenny Uglow
Théophile Gautier	*The Jinx*	Gilbert Adair
André Gide	*Theseus*	
Johann Wolfgang von Goethe	*The Man of Fifty*	A.S. Byatt
Nikolai Gogol	*The Squabble*	Patrick McCabe
E.T.A. Hoffmann	*Mademoiselle de Scudéri*	Gilbert Adair
Victor Hugo	*The Last Day of a Condemned Man*	Libby Purves
Joris-Karl Huysmans	*With the Flow*	Simon Callow
Henry James	*In the Cage*	Libby Purves
Franz Kafka	*Metamorphosis*	Martin Jarvis
Franz Kafka	*The Trial*	Zadie Smith
John Keats	*Fugitive Poems*	Andrew Motion
Heinrich von Kleist	*The Marquise of O–*	Andrew Miller
Mikhail Lermontov	*A Hero of Our Time*	Doris Lessing
Nikolai Leskov	*Lady Macbeth of Mtsensk*	Gilbert Adair
Carlo Levi	*Words are Stones*	Anita Desai
Xavier de Maistre	*A Journey Around my Room*	Alain de Botton
André Malraux	*The Way of the Kings*	Rachel Seiffert
Katherine Mansfield	*Prelude*	William Boyd
Edgar Lee Masters	*Spoon River Anthology*	Shena Mackay
Guy de Maupassant	*Butterball*	Germaine Greer
Prosper Mérimée	*Carmen*	Philip Pullman
Sir Thomas More	*The History of King Richard III*	Sister Wendy Beckett
Sándor Petőfi	*John the Valiant*	George Szirtes

Francis Petrarch	*My Secret Book*	Germaine Greer
Luigi Pirandello	*Loveless Love*	
Edgar Allan Poe	*Eureka*	Sir Patrick Moore
Alexander Pope	*The Rape of the Lock and A Key to the Lock*	Peter Ackroyd
Antoine-François Prévost	*Manon Lescaut*	Germaine Greer
Marcel Proust	*Pleasures and Days*	A.N. Wilson
Alexander Pushkin	*Dubrovsky*	Patrick Neate
Alexander Pushkin	*Ruslan and Lyudmila*	Colm Tóibín
François Rabelais	*Pantagruel*	Paul Bailey
François Rabelais	*Gargantua*	Paul Bailey
Christina Rossetti	*Commonplace*	Andrew Motion
George Sand	*The Devil's Pool*	Victoria Glendinning
Jean-Paul Sartre	*The Wall*	Justin Cartwright
Friedrich von Schiller	*The Ghost-seer*	Martin Jarvis
Mary Shelley	*Transformation*	
Percy Bysshe Shelley	*Zastrozzi*	Germaine Greer
Stendhal	*Memoirs of an Egotist*	Doris Lessing
Robert Louis Stevenson	*Dr Jekyll and Mr Hyde*	Helen Dunmore
Theodor Storm	*The Lake of the Bees*	Alan Sillitoe
Leo Tolstoy	*The Death of Ivan Ilych*	
Leo Tolstoy	*Hadji Murat*	Colm Tóibín
Ivan Turgenev	*Faust*	Simon Callow
Mark Twain	*The Diary of Adam and Eve*	John Updike
Mark Twain	*Tom Sawyer, Detective*	
Oscar Wilde	*The Portrait of Mr W.H.*	Peter Ackroyd
Virginia Woolf	*Carlyle's House and Other Sketches*	Doris Lessing
Virginia Woolf	*Monday or Tuesday*	Scarlett Thomas
Emile Zola	*For a Night of Love*	A.N. Wilson